Q 180.55 .P7 F75 2000
OCLC: 41871668
Writing successful science
proposals

P9-DGE-145

DATE DUE

JAN − 3 2001	
MAR 23 2003	
APR 13 2003	
APR 18 2003	
APR 14 2005	
MAR 2 9 2005	

GAYLORD   PRINTED IN U.S

THE RICHARD STOCKTON COLLEGE
OF NEW JERSEY LIBRARY
POMONA, NEW JERSEY 08240

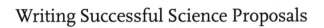

Writing Successful Science Proposals

Writing
Successful
Science
Proposals

Andrew J. Friedland and Carol L. Folt

YALE UNIVERSITY PRESS   New Haven & London

THE RICHARD STOCKTON COLLEGE
OF NEW JERSEY LIBRARY
POMONA, NEW JERSEY 08240

Copyright © 2000 by Yale University.
All rights reserved.
This book may not be reproduced, in whole or in part, including
illustrations, in any form (beyond that copying permitted by
Sections 107 and 108 of the U.S. Copyright Law and except by
reviewers for the public press), without written permission from
the publishers.

Designed by James Johnson and set in Scala Roman type by
The Composing Room of Michigan, Inc., Grand Rapids, Michigan.
Printed in the United States of America by Vail-Ballou Press,
Binghamton, New York.

Library of Congress Cataloging-in-Publication Data

Friedland, Andrew J., 1959–
Writing successful science proposals / Andrew J.
Friedland and Carol L. Folt.
p.   cm.
Includes bibliographical references and index.
ISBN 0-300-08140-5 (cloth : alk. paper). — ISBN 0-300-08141-3
(pbk. : alk. paper)

1. Proposal writing in research.   I. Folt, Carol L., 1951–
II. Title.
Q180.55.P7F75   2000
001.4'4—dc21   99-38996

A catalogue record for this book is available from the British Library.

The paper in this book meets the guidelines for permanence and
durability of the Committee on Production Guidelines for Book
Longevity of the Council on Library Resources.

10 9 8 7 6 5 4 3 2 1

Contents

Preface

One of the most challenging aspects of scientific research is synthesizing past work, current findings, and
new hypotheses into research proposals for future investigations. Such research proposals combine every
aspect of scientific inquiry, from the creative conceptu-
alization to the detailed design, projected analysis of
the data, synthesis of the results, and estimation of the
budget. Because grant applications are an articulation
of the scientific process, writing them is one of the
most exciting parts of "doing science." If you are planning to write a grant application for a major foundation, such as the National Science Foundation, the Environmental Protection Agency, or perhaps a private
foundation, or if you are writing a proposal to conduct
research as a graduate student or undergraduate, this
book should be of value to you.

   Many research institutions offer graduate-level

courses on proposal development, and research design
is growing increasingly vital in the undergraduate science curriculum. Given the importance of this subject
to future scientists, our faculty in ecology and environmental studies at Dartmouth College felt that it was essential that we create a course on scientific project design and proposal writing for our graduate students. In
1994, when we began teaching the course, we could
not find a text that specifically addressed grant writing
in the natural sciences. So we decided to write one our-
selves based on our experiences in the classroom. We
hope that our book will be of value not only to students
but also to new researchers seeking to improve their
skills in developing research proposals.

　　This book provides guidance for those conceptualizing and formulating their research plans, and it
offers specific instruction on organizing and presenting material in a standard format. We offer an overall
organizational framework, and we list the components
of successful scientific proposals. Before you begin to
write, you must have a very clear idea or concept for
your research. There is, however, no secret formula for
writing such proposals. Each grant application must be
tailored to the specifications of the funding agency or
graduate committee to which it is directed.

　　Research proposals are written for a variety of

purposes and are submitted to many different agencies and to faculty committees. We focus on agencies that solicit proposals in the natural sciences; these include the National Science Foundation (NSF), National Institutes of Health (NIH), Environmental Protection Agency (EPA), U.S. Forest Service (USFS), U.S. Geological Survey (USGS), and private corporations and foundations, as well as academic committees. Our format should also be useful to those submitting to the National Research Council of Canada, NATO Scientific and Environmental Affairs Division, and other funding agencies worldwide.

There are many ways to write excellent proposals. We present a model that we and our students and colleagues have used with success. Our ideas have been combined with those of the many natural scientists from a variety of disciplines with whom we have consulted while writing this book. Discussions with colleagues, proposals given to us by successful authors in a variety of fields, and our students' ideas have been especially meaningful in this effort. If you submit a proposal after using this book, or if you use this book in a course, please let us know how you fare. We look forward to hearing from you.

Acknowledgments

We are grateful to the many students, colleagues, advisers, reviewers, and program managers who have contributed greatly to our proposals over the years or directly to this project. While we were writing this book, a number of people generously shared ideas, experiences, and proposals with us. We hope that the following list includes everyone with whom we have communicated. Our sincere apologies for any omissions: John Aber, Victor Ambros, Matt Ayres, Joel Blum, Doug Bolger, Rick Boyce, C. Page Chamberlain, Celia Chen, Jim Coleman, Mary Lou Guerinot, Nelson Hairston, Jr., Dick Holmes, Mary Hudson, Tom Jack, Kevin Kirk, Eric Lambie, Pat McDowell, Mark McPeek, Frank Magilligan, Eric Miller, William North, David Peart, Bill Reiners, Jim Reynolds, Roger Smith, Richard Stemberger, Judy Stern, Ross Virginia, Wayne Wurtsbaugh, and four anonymous reviewers.

Our special thanks to Noel Perrin and Donella Meadows for advice on navigating the publishing world. Graham Herrick contributed a range of ideas and technical assistance. Margaret Dyer Chamberlain provided many cartoons for our consideration. Finally, we thank David Peart, Noel Perrin, and two anonymous reviewers for carefully reading versions of the manuscript, Heidi Downey for valuable editorial assistance, and Jean Thomson Black for her support, enthusiasm, and hard work as our editor.

Writing Successful Science Proposals

A Note to the Reader

We recommend that you read this book in its entirety
before beginning a project. Then review chapter by
chapter—not necessarily in sequence—as you develop
specific sections of your proposal. The following list
contains a number of goals that you can realistically
expect to accomplish over the course of preparing a
research proposal.

- Identify and describe the conceptual framework for the research question.

- Review the relevant theoretical and empirical
  literature both for the system being studied and
  for related systems.

- Articulate the general research question in the
  context of the conceptual framework and the
  theoretical and empirical work that precedes
  the proposed work.

- Formulate a set of hypotheses to address the general question.

- Design studies to test each hypothesis.

- Develop methods and techniques to test, analyze, and synthesize results.

- Evaluate potential alternative outcomes that may be obtained from each part of a study, and consider where each of these alternatives may lead.

- Combine these items in a coherent, precise, concise, exciting proposal.

- Submit the proposal to the appropriate agency or evaluation committee.

- Interpret and respond to reviews of the proposal.

This primer contains a collection of chapters that address our dual goals of assisting development of research ideas and of providing detailed guidelines for writing grant applications. We present the material in much the same order we use in teaching our course, Design and Development of Scientific Proposals, and in designing our own research proposals. We first discuss general types of proposals and share thoughts

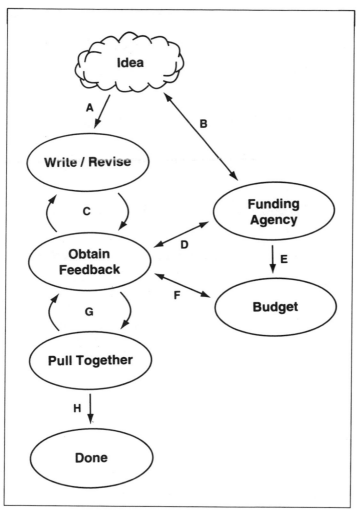

An idea begins the proposal development and writing process, but sometimes a request for proposals from a particular agency can influence or motivate a project. From the original idea in its written form, scientists, funding agency personnel, and agency or budgetary guidelines and restrictions can provide inputs that the writer uses to revise the proposal. After reconciling all comments and feedback, the author submits the final document.

about writing research (Chapters 1 and 2), and then we outline the basic elements of a proposal (Chapter 3). We address the conceptual framework (Chapter 4) and how and where in the grant to articulate succinctly the study's importance. In Chapters 5–13, we address the requirements and construction of the specific elements in a grant proposal (summary, background, methods, budget). We conclude by presenting the mechanics of submitting and tracking a proposal, and by sharing some thoughts about ethics and scientific research (Chapters 14–16).

Getting Started

We vividly remember the intense anticipation that we felt as children at the start of a new school year. Filling our notebooks with stacks of crisp white paper, sharpening our pencils, and buying new books were exciting in large part because we were starting fresh. Anything could happen, and it all could be good! The start of a new year, a new job, a new class, or a new project is a special time, when you feel as if you can accomplish anything.

For many scientists, designing research carries that same sense of exploration, excitement, and unlimited opportunity. For this reason, it is often a scientist's favorite endeavor. As you begin your research proposal, we urge you to:

> **THINK BIG.** Reflect on your problem from its broadest perspective. Imagine finding innova-

tive solutions to fundamentally important problems. If you start small, your work will end up
even smaller.

AVOID TUNNEL VISION. Consider projects
that could lead to years of research. Enjoy a time
of intense creativity, and—at least for a while—
think beyond your immediate research area.

DREAM. Dream about solving important problems, making a difference, producing significant
papers, even winning a Nobel Prize.

TAKE YOUR TIME. Great ideas do not appear
in thirty-minute windows of time. When designing a research project, expect to spend lots of
time on it. You will.

Planning research can be stressful. Anxiety
arises when we focus too much on what people will
think of our work. We all have periods of insecurity,
when we mistakenly believe that everything rests on
the outcome of one specific project. People often fret
about how their advisers or peers will evaluate them.
They worry about their research questions: "Will I
think of a question important enough to keep my interest and warrant my attention for years to come?" They
feel uncertainty about the outcome: "Will my research

idea work?" "Will it lead to publications?" Try not to be overly concerned. Many people experience this when they feel pressured to identify problems.

Reducing the insecurity and uncertainty associated with developing a scientific proposal fosters the excitement and innovation that lie at the heart of science and research design. Here are some simple steps to ease yourself into the process:

- *Define tasks associated with the proposal.* Don't make the list too long or too inclusive at the start, or it will be discouraging.

- *Develop a timeline or strategy for working on your proposal.* Try working backward from your deadline to get a reasonable idea about when specific tasks must be accomplished. Make sure that you have sufficient time.

- *Accomplish something early.* Complete a few tasks quickly. We give our class a set of short- and long-term deadlines at the start of the term. (And we'll present a few examples later in this chapter.)

- *Remember that the best proposals are built from the best science.* Effective proposals require a sound scientific basis. Articulating and developing a logical framework for the problem are

the key elements in the success and power of
the research. Therefore, time spent developing
ideas is well spent. Some researchers believe
that the best problem solvers are individuals
who understand the need to get the initial question right (Runco 1994).

• *Relax, and be prepared for change.* Nothing is
fixed. You will think and rethink everything
throughout the proposal's development.

Exercises for Getting Started

We use three exercises to initiate proposal development. These tasks are not meant to be accomplished in a single sitting but should be pursued con-
currently: critique other proposals; accomplish
administrative and technical tasks; work on the conceptual framework of your research.

Critique other proposals. Established scientists
routinely review the proposals of students and colleagues as part of the peer review process. This gives
them a sense of the scope and size of a research proposal. Assessing other research proposals is also a po-

tent method of learning science and focusing on both the broad implications and the methodology behind research. It is general policy that reviewers destroy proposals after reading them, but most scientists will share their own successful and unsuccessful proposals with peers and students. Do not hesitate to request such assistance from a colleague.

As you read proposals, consider the following major criteria: scientific content, innovation and scope of ideas and methods, structure and format, clarity, and style. Reviewers for the National Science Foundation or other granting agencies may be asked to consider the following while evaluating a proposal: scientific importance of the question(s), rigor of hypotheses, feasibility of research design, qualifications of the investigator, and suitability of facilities for the proposed work.

Our class begins with a discussion of proposals that we have written or that have been given to us by our colleagues to share with the group. Using the title, project summary (or abstract), and significance sections, we question whether the author has convincingly justified the proposed work. We discuss methods, graphics, and style and ask whether the work captured our attention. At some point we try to compare each proposal with others we have read. This discussion is meant to be

a starting point; eventually everyone develops individual
style, methods, and measures for evaluating proposals.

Accomplish administrative tasks. Completing administrative and technical tasks is another effective
way to get started. Begin by reading the proposal guidelines and requirements for the potential funding
agency or foundation, or the guidelines issued by your
department. Fairly early in the process you should put
together a simple outline identifying the key sections
of the final document (see Chapter 3). Think about op-
timal lengths for each section. This activity will probably put you at ease because you will quickly realize that
most grant applications are usually concise—fifteen
single-spaced pages is the maximum for NSF; many
other agencies have the same page limit (dissertation
improvement grants, offered in some programs within
Environmental Biology at NSF, are limited to eight
pages).

Another important task is determining an institution's procedures for grant processing. Ask questions such as, "What paperwork must I complete?"
"What signatures do I need?" "Where do I go?" "How
much time should I allow?" "What are the institution's
rules on budgets, overhead costs, and cost sharing?"
"Do I need special permission for anything?" (e.g., ani-

mal care, use of human subjects). These seemingly mundane points are critical, as poor planning may result in a scramble to meet due dates, or, worse, missed deadlines.

In the past few years, granting agencies have begun to accept electronic submissions, and many do now or will soon require such submissions. For example, many U.S. NSF programs require electronic submission through a program called FastLane. This program allows a researcher to prepare the budget and submit the proposal over the World Wide Web, and it saves on expensive processing and paperwork. As you collect information for submitting a proposal to your potential funding agency, be sure to learn about the requirements regarding electronic submission.

Develop your conceptual framework. Conceptualizing your research is the most substantial step in preparing a proposal. Some people work on their ideas for months or years before they actually begin to write. Others, especially students, pull together their ideas only when they are required to write their first research proposal. In our proposal development class we spend several weeks working to produce a succinct statement of the overall concept that can be understood by a broad scientific audience (see Chapters 4–7). This

statement is the foundation for the rest of the proposal
(see Chapters 8 and 9).

Know Your Audience

Grant applications are written for a variety of
purposes and are submitted to many different types of
agencies. Before you begin writing, consider the fit between your research goals and the targeted agency.
Agencies have various reasons for announcing a Request for Proposals (RFP) or establishing a program
that will periodically accept proposals. In this book we
focus on such agencies as the National Science Foundation (NSF), National Institutes of Health (NIH),
Environmental Protection Agency (EPA), U.S. Forest
Service (USFS), U.S. Geological Survey (USGS), and
private corporations and foundations. For the most
part, we discuss basic research proposals, in which the
investigator sets out research questions and goals.
Agencies sometimes set the goals, however, and request proposals to address a particular objective, research target, or initiative. Accordingly, we separate
proposals into two general categories:

1. **Basic research proposals** (unsolicited research
proposals), which generally must provide novel

LITZLER

"WAS THERE ANY TALK ABOUT FUNDING?"

insights or methodologies for solving fundamental scientific problems (see Chapter 4).

2. Task-oriented or program-initiated proposals are
those in which the topic or goal of research is
specified by an agency, a corporation, or a foundation.

There is usually less latitude in determining research topics than for basic research proposals.
Proposals are evaluated on their likelihood of ac-
complishing the specified task, so emphasis is
placed on methods, ability to accomplish the
project, credentials, the projected outputs, and
time needed to complete the project. (These criteria are also important in basic research proposals.)

Once you have identified a specific program or
agency and become familiar with the guidelines, talk
with the program director or manager (the person in
charge of evaluating grants in that program). Do not
call until you have definite questions. Avoid open-
ended queries, such as, "What kind of proposals do you
fund?" Take notes during the conversation. Discuss the
goals and general format of your project and ask such
questions as, "Does my proposed research fit within

the mandate of your program?" "Is there a related program that you think would be better suited to evaluate my project?" There may be unwritten requirements for successful grants that you need to clarify with the program director. For example, you may wish to address a question by comparing data from diverse regions around the world, but the agency may be interested only in questions about a particular region. The program manager can clarify such issues relating to the scope of the program. Be sure to ask about spending limits, restrictions on equipment purchases and investigator salaries, and other financial regulations. (See also Chapter 13.)

It is also appropriate to ask the program manager about the review process. Find out the backgrounds of the scientists who will evaluate your application. By knowing your audience, you can anticipate their questions and address likely concerns in the proposal. For proposals that cross disciplinary boundaries, this information is critical. When conducting interdisciplinary research you will need to address the concerns of individuals in each discipline. Discussions with the program director and with scientists in the pertinent fields will save you much time and effort and could make the difference between success and failure.

LITZLER

"AS WE CONSIDER THE PROPOSALS, LET'S NOT FORGET WHO INCLUDED A GALLON OF ROCKY ROAD AS 'ATTACHMENT B'."

Other Exercises for Getting Started

- Distinguish tasks that can be accomplished in one or two days from longer-term chores.

- Find at least one set of proposal guidelines. This can be accomplished by contacting the office on your campus that handles the submission and administration of grant awards, surfing the Internet for agencies' guidelines, or borrowing from a colleague or adviser. See the Web addresses for funding agencies in appendix 2.

- Begin to identify specific sections required in the final proposal and to list the elements they should contain.

CHAPTER 2

Authorship from
Start to Finish

Responsibility for research extends from conception and completion of a proposal to publication and future use of the resulting data. The individuals who accept this responsibility—and the credit for the ideas, methodologies, and eventual results developed in a proposal—are the authors of that proposal. Sometimes authorship is shared, and coauthorship of grants usually leads to coauthorship of the resulting publications. Because students often find authorship a difficult and uncertain topic, we discuss it near the start of our proposal development class.

There are two essential points to consider about authorship:

- *Discuss expectations.* Determine in advance specific expectations for each author and collaborator for all phases of proposal development and research implementation. This includes authorship and revision of publications resulting from a research project.

• *Appreciate all that goes into research.* Understand the components of designing, conducting, analyzing, and writing scientific research. Fully acknowledge sources of supporting information, derivative ideas, and collaborators. As this understanding and appreciation develop, authorship decisions will be made appropriately, and there will be fewer chances for misunderstanding.

Define Expectations at the Outset

Scientific advances are best achieved through honest sharing of ideas, constructive critical appraisal by colleagues, and revisions in approaches and perspectives resulting from these debates. Science is always collaborative at some level, and as such it requires trust and understanding among associates. Be generous with your feedback to others and you will benefit as well. Don't let fears of having your ideas taken without credit diminish your relationships with collaborators and colleagues. The most effective strategy for avoiding problems over collaboration and authorship is to establish, at the start, clear expectations for all members of a project.

Who is the first author and what does the first author do? Every author on a proposal or paper has assumed ethical and fiscal responsibility for the research project. The first author on a funded project, the principal investigator (PI), takes primary responsibility for the project (cf. Day 1988). This author often does the most work toward the conception and implementation of the project, although some projects may be conceived by one person and carried out and expanded by another.

For certain proposals, the first author and presence or absence of collaborators are mandated by the funding agency or review committee. For example, proposals submitted by graduate students to dissertation committees usually carry only the student's name. However, the adviser probably had a guiding role in the proposal; a later application to an outside agency may well be cowritten by the student and the adviser. Some funding programs (such as NSF dissertation improvement grants) require that the PI on grants be a faculty member at a research institution or an accredited college or university. This policy may exist in order to ensure that applicants have scientific training and experience; it also directs fiscal and ethical responsibility to a defined individual. These types of requirements are usually discussed under a section describing eligibility for specific grants.

Sources versus collaborators. Aside from "obvious" associations (e.g., between advisers and students, between long-standing research collaborators, and between co-writers), co-investigators are usually added to a proposal when their expertise is required for the research. If you have a casual conversation with someone and provide a good idea that he or she later uses, you should be flattered. You may be acknowledged, but your suggestion may not entitle you to participate in the project. Interactive scientists make suggestions about other people's research all the time; if your suggestions are good, they will be used frequently, but they may seldom lead to collaboration.

Being a co-investigator on a grant application generally implies a long-term contribution to the ideas, design, implementation, data analysis, and future publications. Each case should be decided on its own merits, but early discussion of this issue is warranted.

Appreciate All That Goes into Research and Give Credit Where Credit Is Due

You should discuss authorship of possible publications even as the proposal is being written. Inherent in such discussion is an expectation that the research will be taken seriously, be executed well, and be interesting enough to merit publication. You and your collaborators will probably return to this discussion several times after the research design is complete.

To give proper credit and to determine authorship of eventual publications, you must recognize the importance of all contributions to the scientific research. This understanding is also critical for writing a proposal and determining how and when tasks will be performed. Less experienced researchers may feel that the most important contributions come from those who physically collect the data. But even though data collection is important, participation in the following areas may be even more critical to the outcome of the research, and it could lead to first authorship of eventual papers:

- identification of research problems
- design of effective research protocols

- sample analysis

- data analysis

- writing the document

If you and your collaborators discuss authorship early you will avoid misunderstandings later. This discussion may also help guide decisions about who will do key pieces of the project and about the timeline for project completion, which will facilitate the success of the research effort.

No One Owns Ideas. Right?

Research is not about ownership, but about sharing. Yet we all have assumptions regarding who gets to use project data and publish the results. Normally the investigators of a project have sole access to the first use and publication of data. After results are published, they can be used by anyone who properly cites the published work. Funding agencies may require that investigators make data accessible to the public via the Internet. Some agencies require that all data be made available within a certain time period, whether or not the data have been published.

Different disciplines have different protocols

and practices. Laws regarding intellectual property
rights and patents apply in some areas of science and
not in others. If there are any questions about the ownership of ideas, techniques, or instruments you may
develop, contact your institution's grants administration office.

Difficulties can arise if collaborators have not
anticipated what will happen to research and data after
a proposed project is completed. It is particularly important to discuss this issue with students, postdoctoral fellows, and other research associates before beginning a collaborative project. The following
examples illustrate common situations in which research may be expected to "stay within a lab" (i.e., under a specific laboratory director or PI) after the primary researcher (e.g., a graduate student, technician,
research associate) on that project leaves the lab.

Longitudinal studies (studies that follow specific
individuals or sites over time). The value of longitudinal studies grows over time, and the initial data base often yields additional research. Examples of longitudinal data bases include individuals being observed after
exposure to some factor (e.g., pollutants, drugs, haz-
ards); plots of trees being followed from seedling stage
through maturity; or repeated visits (perhaps once per
decade) to sample soils or sediments. In most cases,

the investigators who designed, arranged to fund, and executed an original study control access beyond the initial grant by continuing to maintain the research sites or follow the individuals studied. A student or co-investigator who joins a project with specific objectives for use of the original sites or individuals should not assume that future access is guaranteed.

Laboratory study systems. In some fields it is common for students and postdoctoral fellows to conduct research on systems (e.g., specific genes or gene products) that have been identified, described, and manufactured by previous "generations" of scientists in the same lab. Scientists training in these laboratories usually leave their project behind when they depart from a lab; they develop new systems (separate from their thesis work) when they assume positions elsewhere.

Technique and instrumentation development. For many scientists, developing new techniques and applying sophisticated instrumentation to novel problems are primary research objectives. Individuals who use these techniques or rely on instrumentation developed and maintained by others cannot assume that they will have future access to and involvement with the instrument or techniques.

We urge you to discuss this issue in advance with advisers, colleagues, and collaborators. Understand the culture of each field with respect to this idea. If you are uncomfortable with the prospects, discuss them with the appropriate people early in the project. Don't assume that you can agree now and change the expectations later.

One of us was involved with five graduate students and faculty members in a large project. Early in the project we wrote down the area in which each person would assume responsibility for doing research, writing, and revising. We even wrote the potential titles of resulting papers and listed the journals in which we intended to publish. Five years later, much of the work had been completed and most of the papers had been written, and there was little debate about who would be the lead author on each paper. We ascribed this consensus, in part, to our identifying the "ownership" of the different parts of the project early in its development.

Exercises for Authorship

The best preparation for thinking about authorship of proposals and papers is to share opinions about this topic with your adviser or colleagues. We have an

annual seminar with our graduate students on this issue, and it is always thought-provoking and interesting
for the participants.

Read the following sequence of scenarios and
discuss your expectations for collaboration or eventual
authorship.

- You have developed a set of hypotheses to test
  in a system you know quite well. You present
  your ideas at an informal department gather-
  ing. A colleague brings to your attention a particular paper that describes an appropriate
  method. What should you do? If you use the
  method in your eventual design, what does
  your colleague expect in the way of recognition?

- Now, consider a situation in which the methodology needed for conducting your tests does not
  exist or requires a method being developed by a
  colleague. In this situation, suppose the colleague suggests a way to achieve your goal, or
  states that she could develop a method that
  would meet your needs. What should you do?
  If, in your eventual design, you use the method
  she develops, what do you and your colleague
  expect about her recognition?

- Finally, consider a situation in which you develop a series of ideas on how to test your hypotheses as a result of a number of late-night and hallway chats held over weeks or months with a particular colleague. What if your colleague's perception of how much help you received differs from yours? In this scenario, a misunderstanding may easily occur. What should you do?

Basic Organization and Effective Communication

Many novice writers find it difficult to decide on an organizational structure for their proposal. The number of sections and the disparate types of information that must be included can be overwhelming. Although the key to a good proposal is sound science, efficient organization makes a scientifically convincing project even stronger.

Some funding agencies are flexible in their specifications for proposal format. Others require that sections be presented in a particular sequence. Our recommendations in this chapter are based on the format suggested by the U.S. National Science Foundation in the Grant Proposal Guide (currently referred to by NSF as GPG, NSF 99–2; be sure to use the most up-to-date version).

Four Precepts for Effective Organization and Communication

Effective communication substantially im-
proves your chances of success. If your language is
clear and precise, and your document well organized,
your ideas will be better understood, their importance
will be more apparent, and the comments of reviewers
will be more useful. We propose four axioms for com-
municating your ideas: *organize, highlight, funnel,* and
focus. A well-*organized* document is easier to follow
and comprehend. *Highlight* your most important
points early in your proposal. This directs the reader
toward the issues that you feel are vital and thereby
increases your impact. Do not emphasize ideas that are
less important to your research, and do not bury critical
information. Whenever possible, *funnel* the reader
from the big picture to the specifics of your research.
Then *focus* on that topic—avoid information that de-
tracts from or dilutes your message. Funneling and focusing establish that your project is the obvious, logical
way to answer the questions you raise. Finally, offer the
readers a "road map" early in the proposal (and often in
each section) to keep them headed in the direction you
wish.

Organizing a Proposal for the NSF

The National Science Foundation is an independent federal agency mandated to promote and advance scientific and engineering progress in the United States. The foundation receives more than thirty thousand proposals annually and makes about ten thousand new awards (NSF Grant Proposal Guide, 1998, p. i). However, many competitive programs within NSF fund 20 percent or fewer of the proposals they receive.

The GPG, which is free, is a very useful document for proposal writing. The guide is valuable for anyone working on a proposal, even if a proposal is not for submission to NSF, because it clearly specifies typical research proposal expectations. For a copy of the GPG, access NSF on the Internet at http://www.nsf.gov. Or write to NSF, 4201 Wilson Boulevard, Arlington, VA 22230.

Many types of proposals are submitted to NSF, but we focus here on the so-called Unsolicited Research Proposals. These are basic research proposals that can be submitted to NSF in topic areas, called directorates, from geosciences, mathematical and physical sciences, engineering, biological sciences, and social, behavioral, and economic sciences. Within these and other directorates are perhaps 250 programs (for example, within the directorate for biological sciences there is a division of molecular and cellular biosciences and a program called cell biology; within the directorate for geosciences is a division of earth sciences and a program on hydrologic sciences).

The NSF tells you that the "proposal should present the: (1) objectives and scientific or educational significance of the proposed work, (2) the suitability of the methods to be employed, (3) qualifications of the investigator and the grantee organization, (4) effects of the activity on the infrastructure of science, engineering and education, and (5) amount of funding required. It should present the merits of the proposed project clearly and should be prepared with the care and thoroughness of a paper submitted for publication" (GPG, p. 1).

Note that the NSF's statement does not identify specific sections or a particular order for the proposal. It does, however, highlight key criteria that NSF reviewers use to evaluate applications:

- General implications of your research (item 1)

- The strength of your argument for funding (items 1 and 5)

• Scientific soundness, fundamental importance, possibility for far-reaching impact, investigator qualifications, and strong likelihood that
the project will advance research efforts in a
discipline

A "typical" NSF proposal includes the following
sections in this general order:

1. Project summary (or abstract)

2. Table of contents

3. Project description (this is the main body of
   the proposal [see table 1]; order is not specified
   by NSF)

4. Reference list

5. Biographical sketches of the investigator(s)

6. Budget

7. Current and pending support of the investigators

8. Description of the facilities, equipment, and
   other resources available for use

Other organizations may have different specific
requirements, but most include roughly the same ele-

ments. The balance of the proposal can vary among agencies, with respect to detail or emphasis on sections such as experimental protocol. Moreover, a few agencies require additional components, such as quality assurance information, special permits, or cooperative agreements. You will need to obtain this information from the program director.

Some programs require particular headings and a fixed order of presentation. For NSF, the overall sequence is prescribed, but within the body of the proposal the investigator has much latitude concerning the actual contents, names, and placement of sections. If your proposal is a resubmission, some review panels also suggest or require a "resubmission response" in the main body of the proposal (see Chapter 15).

In the following chapters we provide more detail on each section. An outline of the sections that constitute the body of the research description is shown below. Some writers do not use all of these sections, whereas others use more. Ask colleagues or advisers who have received funding to let you read their successful proposals.

Sections commonly found in proposals. Chapter numbers shown in parentheses are references to this book.

Pitfalls

Perhaps the most common conceptual pitfall is the failure to establish the general significance of your work or to link it logically to your project. Another typical error is devoting too much text to complex details or to your past accomplishments. Unless these are pertinent to your study, you could lose the attention of reviewers. Other widespread weaknesses include a failure to construct *testable* hypotheses; the construction of too many hypotheses; bad analytical or statistical methods; poor experimental design; weak questions; good big picture but inappropriate tests for that question; too ambitious a project for the time and money requested; inadequate skills or credentials for the task proposed. Finally, there are a number of procedural pitfalls that are to be avoided at all costs. Most of these are obvious but can be critical. For example, avoid alienating the reviewers by permitting typographical errors, erroneous references, or incorrect or inconsistent numbers to creep into the text. Follow all page length guidelines! Present a pleasant-looking document that is legible and logical and, whenever possible, reader friendly. Again, evaluating other proposals and looking at your own project with these specific issues in mind is of great benefit throughout the writing process.

C H A P T E R   4

Developing Your Conceptual Framework and Significance Statement

Scientific proposals are always judged by their perceived significance. This is true whether you are writing for the NSF, the American Heart Association, a local conservation society, or a dissertation committee. Everyone who funds or supervises research inevitably asks what makes the proposed research "significant." If you cannot answer this question, stop writing and keep thinking.

All of the scientists we asked agreed that time spent early developing a proposal's significance, objectives, and hypotheses is time well spent. Remember that persuasive questions are essential for successful proposals.

Four cornerstones underlying good research are:

- Important questions

- The best and most appropriate methods

- Appropriate analysis and application of results

- Synthesis and timely dissemination of results

In this chapter we provide suggestions for conceptualizing and developing the first of these cornerstones, and offer simple guidelines for writing a compelling significance section and placing it strategically
in your research proposal.

Developing Your
Significance Statement

The questions to be addressed by the study generally are featured with their justification in a significance section. Many scientists feel that this is the most
important piece of a research proposal. A well-written
significance section highlights the fundamental value
of the proposed research, so we suggest that you start
the research unit with a significance section (see also
Chapter 3). This section should be linked to the specific

"I'M AT THAT AWKWARD STAGE IN THE PROPOSAL WHERE I HAVE TO ASK FOR SOMETHING."

objectives and hypotheses (discussed in Chapter 7) of your study, which should follow closely in the proposal. The reviewer must find that the logic in this section is sound, that the ideas are exciting, and that the scope is reasonable within the time and budget you propose. Obviously this is not a trivial job.

To refine your thinking on the significance of your research, step outside your own discipline and immediate needs and take a broad and long-term view of your research. This perspective is essential for building a valuable and wide-reaching set of hypotheses. The goal is to end up with a pithy and accurate statement of the significance before you write the section. While writing or evaluating the significance section of a proposal we suggest that you:

- Look at the project from both a broad and narrow disciplinary view.

- Ask what scientists *inside* versus *outside* the field would perceive as the greatest contribution of this research.

- Consider both the empirical and theoretical contributions that may result from the study.

- Identify and contrast basic and applied uses of the data.

- Ask how you most expect and hope your research will be used by others.

- Compare contributions of the project that are likely to be important one year versus ten years after the completion of the project. Remember that the significance of a project changes with time and new technologies.

- Be your own best critic and ask how an impartial reader would dispute the claims that you have made.

Exercises for Developing Your Significance Statement

The following exercises help you to conceptualize and articulate your research proposals *before* you begin to write. View these drills as the building blocks for writing the entire proposal, and follow the four precepts for effective communication (organize, highlight, funnel, and focus) while doing them.

EXERCISE 1: Prepare a ten- to fifteen-minute oral presentation of the conceptual framework for your proposal. Restrict yourself to the use of three overhead transparencies. The challenge is to present the conceptual framework without reference to any specific system. For example, suppose you plan to investigate synergistic effects of exposure to toxic metals on reproduction and growth of oysters in estuaries off the Maine coast. For this exercise, distill the key conceptual points of your proposal: those ideas that are of importance *beyond* oysters, the specific metals you'll study, and estuaries in Maine. For example, you could focus on understanding syngerisms among contaminants that occur in combination. The point of departure for your talk could be the need to tease apart mechanisms of interactions among contaminants in order to devise remediation strategies.

This activity forces you to articulate your general research question in broad terms, and to relate your study to the theoretical and empirical research that precedes it. If you must use a system to illustrate aspects of the discussion, do *not* use the system you intend to study. If you are doing this as a written exercise, confine your writing to a single page.

EXERCISE 2: Distill your previous presentation to a five- to ten-minute oral presentation of the significance and broad objectives of your research. This time you can refer to the specific system, cells, or organisms that you actually plan to study. When you can do this effectively you are probably ready to write a project summary and a brief yet pointed introductory significance statement for your proposal (see Chapter 6).

EXERCISE 3: Prepare a ten- to fifteen-minute presentation of the conceptual framework for your research project, focusing on the underlying quantitative, theoretical, and functional relations. Proposals often include or require a model or series of models to identify the key relations between processes (see Chapter 8). As in exercises 1 and 2, emphasize the relation between your study and the theoretical and empirical research preceding it. This exercise is usually accompanied by a graphic presentation of the conceptual or quantitative relations. Successful completion of this exercise can produce a piece to be used in the introduction and justification of your study.

EXERCISE 4: Identify a system (e.g., biochemical process, species, habitat) that is as analogous to the one you plan to study as possible. Give another five-minute oral presentation (or prepare a one-page written summary) on the significance and broad objectives of your research, this time structured entirely around the comparable system. This exercise forces you to consider the relations between significance and specific objectives more precisely, because sometimes objectives may not be as generally applicable as believed. This may make you reevaluate your objectives with respect to your chosen study system.

Crafting the
Significance Statement

An effective, engaging significance section motivates the reader to give your proposal a thorough appraisal, and it establishes the framework for the rest of the study. The overall goals and significance should also target information necessary in the background section (Chapter 10) and lead the reviewer directly to the objectives and hypotheses or specific research questions. If the significance section is not consistent with the other sections, your proposal will not be persuasive.

A formulaic approach is rarely wise, yet we agree with the widely held philosophy that an effective significance section (generally one to two pages) begins with the "big picture" motivating your work, elaborates on the scientific context for your study, describes briefly your own research plans, and restates the overall goals and expected results. Here are several tips for producing your significance section, compiled from our reviews of a number of excellent proposals.

- *Feature the significance section at the start of the proposal.* This allows you to set the tone for the entire proposal. Some people place the significance section at the end of the proposal, but we find that this is much less effective. By that point most reviewers will have already formed a firm opinion of the study.

- *Keep the section short.* Don't dilute your message with detail, but be sure to elaborate beyond the project summary (see Chapter 6).

- *Funnel the reader.* Take the reader from your broadest goals to your specific aims. The more effective your funnel, the clearer the section will be. If you can write a statement in which your research appears to be the most logical and innovative approach to answering the question raised in the first or second sentence, you will have accomplished a great deal.

- *Explain the value of your work.* It is essential that you explain the value of your research questions in a manner that is accessible and convincing to scientists both in and out of your immediate discipline. Perhaps you have identified a glaring gap in knowledge. If so, explain what information is missing and describe how finding that information may lead to other important research. Maybe you plan to work on a process that has been identified in one system but not tested in other systems. You must convince the reader that testing the process in another system is important in some fundamental way. After reviewing this section the reader should understand how the successful completion of your work will advance the state of science in your field.

• *Link with other fields.* Successful research usually has significance beyond its immediate domain. Briefly explain the implications of your work for other fields, and how it can be applied in those fields. This makes your work more appealing, and it emphasizes that your study has breadth.

• *Don't go overboard.* One important note of caution—be sure not to overreach. Reviewers become annoyed if the claims for significance are out of proportion to the research.

You can accomplish your task in a variety of ways. When composing the significance section, people often go back and forth between significance, objectives, and methods. We usually first write a rough draft of the significance section, develop the objectives and hypotheses, consider the methods, and then reconsider and rewrite the significance section. When writing this section, remind yourself of some often-encountered pitfalls: language that is too vague, use of overblown or naive statements of significance, repetition of other sections without additional detail, and confusing or jargon-heavy language that fails to engage the reader. As we stated earlier, it is usually most effective to delay writing until you have completed the thinking for this section and read a number of proposals in your discipline.

More Exercises for Writing the Significance Section

To help hone your skills, we suggest that you critique the significance paragraphs of other proposals. We do this in the classroom, using a supply of proposals given to us by their authors. With our students we evaluate the effectiveness of significance sections based on content, perceived importance of the questions, placement in the grant, basic writing skills, and style. This activity is valuable at any time in the development of a proposal.

Experiment with names for this section. Different titles are commonly used. Some are more forceful than others, depending on the type and objectives of the proposal. Here are some examples from successful proposals. Which do you prefer?

- Overall Objectives
- Overview and Significance
- Significance and Project Objectives
- Statement of the Problem

Critique other significance sections. Consider the following excerpts from three significance sections and one entire significance section. Are they cogent? Are you engaged? Do they successfully cover some of the points listed above? Are the primary pitfalls avoided?

Field Measurements of Phytochelatins* in Crops and Ecosystems Contaminated by Metals

Understanding how metal pollutants affect crops and forests is obviously of great importance to U.S. agriculture. Much research is aimed at elucidating the mechanisms of plant-metal interactions, including the induction of phytochelatins.

Source: F. M. M. Morel, excerpted from the Rationale and Significance section

*Phytochelatins are peptides, naturally produced by plants, that bind metals

Quantification of Base Cation Sources and Cycling in a Forest Ecosystem Using Strontium Isotope Tracers and Mass Balance Methods

The proposed research should yield new estimates of internal ecosystem cation fluxes such as canopy leaching and release during organic matter decomposition. These elemental transfers are generally determined as the residuals in mass balance studies. Strontium isotopic tracer methods will provide independent estimates of these important cation fluxes. . . .

The results of our proposed research will be applicable to the greater Adirondack Mountain area as anorthositic and granitic rocks are the major parent materials in this region. . . .

Source: E. Miller, A. Friedland and J. Blum, excerpted from the Significance section

Understanding Hydraulic Conductivity in Aquifers from Above-ground Measurements

Understanding hydraulic conductivity of a variety of aquifers has global importance and cannot be undervalued given the enormity of environmental problems related to contamination of aquifers. Our proposed technique, if successful, has the potential to revolutionize the way that groundwater studies are conducted. It may also greatly affect the rates of species extinction, global warming, and frequency of El Niño events.

Source: Excerpted from the Significance section of a fictional proposal

Do you think that the relative weights given to justification of the big picture and its link to the aims of the study are effective in the following example?

Metal Accumulation in Aquatic Organisms

Metals enter aquatic food webs in several ways, ranging from atmospheric deposition to surface or groundwater flow of metal enriched water. Once in lakes, metals become incorporated in the food web via direct uptake from the water or the ingestion of metal-bearing foods. Large changes in species composition, species diversity, biomass, and growth of aquatic organisms have been measured in metal-impacted lakes. In some lakes, fisheries have declined seriously and the accumulation of metals in fish tissue has been recognized widely as a human health hazard. Mercury is of special concern, because elevated levels of mercury have been found in fish from a large number of lakes in remote areas not associated with local sources of contamination.

Aquatic organisms accumulate metals in their tissues from their diet. Bioaccumulation is the general process by which metals are taken up directly from the water and the food. Biomagnification describes a systematic increase in the concentration of metals (or other chemicals like DDT and PCBs) in tissue as the chemical moves up a trophic food web (i.e., from algae to zooplankton to fish). Not all metals biomagnify, but all do bioaccumulate. Metals such as lead and cadmium bioaccumulate, but may not biomagnify. In contrast, mercury bioaccumulates and biomagnifies, which can result in very high concentrations of mercury in fish from lakes with low mercury levels in the water.

Complex biological mechanisms and relationships make it impossible to simply predict the risk of exposure to metals from the metal concentration in the water. Prior studies on bioaccumulation and biomagnification of metals have shown that the differences in the concentration of metal in fish tissue (body burden) result from species- and age-specific behavioral and physiological traits. For example, species with feeding behaviors that increase exposure (e.g., benthic feeders are highly exposed to metals in sediments) carry higher body burdens. Physiological mechanisms that strip metals reduce body burdens in some species but not others. For metals that biomagnify, the trophic position of the fish has a profound influence on body burden. Predatory fish (high on the food chain) have higher body burdens of mercury than planktivorous fish (lower on the food chain) of equal body size. Hence, the body burden of metals in fish can be understood only by considering the food web relations in lakes.

To date, there are very few lakes for which food web relations, metal concentrations, and body burden values are known. This information is critical for assessing the current level of risk to humans and aquatic organisms and for developing predictive models for the functional relations between such important measures as body burden, food web composition, and water quality. The aims of the proposed study are to measure variation in the bioaccumulation and biomagnification of toxic metals in lakes, with dual goals of understanding effects of hazardous substances on ecological systems, and the role of food web structure in determining bioavailability of metals to humans. Metals with different potential for bioaccumulation and biomagnification will be contrasted. . . .

Source: C. L. Folt, C. Y. Chen, and R. L. Stemberger, modified from the Significance section

Write your own significance section. After you have written a significance section, ask friends and colleagues to read it. Keep in mind the essential points to cover and the pitfalls to avoid. If you have a solid, persuasive significance section, you are well on the way to completing a successful proposal.

CHAPTER 5

A Title May Be More Important Than You Think

Titles are often written at the last minute and typically receive less thought than the rest of the proposal. But the title introduces your reader to the framework and perspective of the document. An effective title will capture that reader's attention and prepare the reader for the focus you wish to establish. The role of the title can be significant during the evaluation process, in which a review committee may collectively assess up to two hundred proposals. In some cases, members of a review committee may start by reading the applications with the most intriguing titles. It is advantageous to get a reviewer's attention when she is freshest and most receptive to new ideas.

Components of a Good Title

The title must encompass the focus or concept of your proposal. If it is too descriptive, it may appear narrow, but if it is too broad, it may appear unachievable. An effective title accurately represents the content of the proposal. Practice is the soundest way to learn how to write a title. Read an assortment of titles, and as you read them, refine your own.

- Present your title in a clear, concise, meaningful manner.

- Avoid jargon and overstatement.

- Consider the impact of using buzzwords. Be aware that such language alienates some readers just as it attracts others.

- Avoid titles that are "cute" or too informal. This is arguably a matter of style, but we prefer titles that leave out the humor.

Exercises for Writing Titles

Ask yourself how your title can be clarified, shortened, and made more precise. Work on your title, share it, and rework it.

Categorize and modify existing titles. Titles come in many forms—questions, descriptions, bold statements. Each form works well in specific situations. Consider the following title: "Bedrock Influence on Soil Chemistry in Western Vermont." This descriptive title gives the reader a fairly good idea of the general topic but does not give any details on the system being studied or the questions being asked. "The Influence of Limestone on Base Saturation in Soils of the Lake Champlain Valley" is more specific, but it may not be immediately clear to nonspecialists. Both titles are more informative than "The Relationship Between Soils and Parent Material." Which of the first two titles is more desirable may depend on the exact content of the proposal, the agency or program to which it is being submitted, and the type of reviewers who are likely to read the proposal (specialists or generalists).

We contrived the following list of titles to represent the variety seen in proposals. Some are modified from published titles. Remember, evaluations are not necessarily conducted by specialists in the same field as the author of the proposal, so titles that can be understood only by a scientist in a particular discipline may not fare well. Most of these titles can be improved. Are they understandable? Is it easy to guess the content of the proposal based on the title? Would a few word

changes or a different approach result in a title that
would be more interesting or effective to a nonspecial-
ist in this discipline?

1. "Does Tectonic Activity Cause Global Extinc-
   tions?"

2. "Temperature and Moisture: Controls on
   Global Carbon Cycles"

3. "Mathematical Modeling of Non-linear Systems"

4. "Mechanisms of Cell Division and Differentiation"

5. "Large Mammal Response to Habitat Frag-
   mentation: Reproduction and Survival Rates
   on Two Continents"

6. "Nutrient Cycling in Freshwater Ponds: The
   Role of Two Fish Species and Three Algae
   Species in Four Lakes"

7. "Molecular Mechanisms and Regulation of
   Metal Ion Uptake in Eukaryotic Cells"

8. "Basic Research for the Future: Are There
   Enough Resources to Support the Human
   Population?"

9. "Erosion in Streams—Slip Sliding Away?"

10. "Influence of Electromagnetic Fields on Bovine Health"

11. "In Search of the Solar Constant"

12. "Source and Fate of Particles in Wastewater Treatment Facilities"

13. "Acidic Permian Lakes: Understanding the Geochemistry of Ancient Acid Systems"

Construct titles from existing project summaries. Summaries (or abstracts) from proposals that have been funded by such government agencies as NSF and NIH are accessible on a variety of Web sites. One suggestion is to take agency-posted entries from the Web and evaluate both the summaries and the titles. Do the titles capture your attention? Do they encapsulate the material outlined in the abstract? You can also write your own titles for these proposals based on the summary.

Here are summaries from two funded grants. Try to write a good title for each. Our students actually drafted titles very close to the originals, which underscores the clarity of these summaries.

Sample 1
The objective of the proposed research is to experimentally investigate the effects of temporal variation in resource supply on the outcome and

dynamics of competition between consumers. The proposed research would use planktonic rotifers (small, multicellular zooplankton) as model systems. Experiments would test the predictions that temporal variation in resource supply changes competitive outcome, slows the rate of competitive exclusion, and allows competing species to coexist. These experiments would go beyond existing experimental studies by combining the following aspects: (1) using multicellular organisms instead of microbes, (2) using a temporal pattern of resource supply that is more realistic than that used in previous experiments, (3) measuring the effect of temporal variation in resource supply on the threshold resource concentration for positive population growth, and (4) predicting changes in competitive outcome, dynamics, and species diversity at different scales of temporal variation.

Source: K. L. Kirk

Sample 2

Overpumping of California's Salinas River Valley aquifers has prompted seawater intrusion, adversely affecting groundwater quality. Consequently, the sustainability of Monterey County agriculture is jeopardized. Growers recognize that the solution to preventing further intrusion lies in regulation of the aquifer, but they differ in their commitment to accepting groundwater upper pumping limits or pumping taxes.

In order to motivate grower effort to manage the groundwater resources more effectively, the effect of one grower's pumping on the water quality and quantity of all other growers should be quantified. Because sea water intrudes the aquifer through diffusion, growers who pump closer to the intruded area cause more damage than those who

pump at the other end of the aquifer, given equal
rates of pumping across growers. This suggests that
a policy that varies by region would be more
effective than a basin-wide policy. We will simulate
present conditions in the aquifer as well as impacts of
policy alternatives through the use of a Geographical
Information System (GIS) computer program.

Source: D. D. Parker

Here are some titles modified slightly from
successful proposals. The actual titles from the two
summaries presented above are at the end of this list.
Notice that almost all of these titles are concise and
clear.

1. "Analysis of Pesticide Transport Pathways
   and Degradation in Natural Wetlands"

2. "The Role of Ecological Interactions in Diver-
   sification: Phylogeny and Population Differentiation of Goldenrod in Two Communities"

3. "Human Modification of Landscape Function in New England and Florida"

4. "Predicting the Response of Terrestrial
   Ecosystems to Elevated CO_2 and Climatic
   Change"

5. "Thermal Conductivity in Oceanic Waters:
   Internal and External Factors"

6. "Patterns and Processes of Geomorphic and Hydraulic Adjustments During Stream Channel Recovery"

7. "Mercury Flux Estimates from Sites to Regions: Scaling-Up Across the Northern Hemisphere"

8. "Role of Plant Transcriptional Adaptors in Heat Shock–Regulated Gene Expression"

9. "Dynamics of the Mesospheres and Lower Thermospheres of the Arctic and Antarctic"

10. "Effects of Plasma Ionization on the Nonlinear Dynamics of Emission Spectrophotometers"

11. "Detailed Dynamics of Atmospheric Photoreactions"

12. "Reconciling Molecular and Fossil Evidence on the Age of Angiosperms"

13. "A Study of the Abundance and $^{13}C/^{12}C$ Ratio of Atmospheric Carbon Dioxide and Oceanic Carbon in Relation to the Global Carbon Cycle"

14. "The Role of Identified Cells in Directional Motor Behavior"

15. "Genetics, Mechanism, and Regulation of Protein Synthesis in *G. hypothetica*"

16. "Segment-Based Acoustic Models for Continuous Pattern Recognition"

17. "Resource Competition Between Rotifers in a Variable Environment"

18. "Spatially Efficient Management of a Sea Water–Intruded Aquifer"

Write and critique your own title. Some people write a title as they begin their proposal, and others wait until the proposal is completed. Reviewers often say that they can tell new grant writers by the titles of their proposals, which tend to be wordy and either highly specific or overblown. Try a number of titles, and experiment with the various forms. Feedback from friends and colleagues is extremely useful.

The Project Summary Guides the Reader

As the first and shortest section in an NSF-type proposal, the project summary serves several vital functions. It is where you frame the goals and scope of your study, briefly describe the methods, and present the hypotheses and expected results or outputs. The project summary (some people use this term synonymously with "abstract") is the initial description of the project seen by reviewers. A convincing and exciting summary captures their attention and interest, and it establishes a strong tone for the entire document. It is critical to set up the proper expectations, to avoid misleading readers into thinking the proposal addresses anything other than the actual topic. What a challenge—to be clear, concise, accurate, and exciting, all in fewer than three hundred words!

When assessing a proposal, reviewers use the

summary as a template or guide to the document. Their impressions of the summary are critical. Program directors frequently rely on the summary when choosing ad hoc reviewers. Summaries also are used later to remind evaluators of the key elements in the design and of the expected outputs. This role is particularly important for proposals being formally evaluated and assessed during panel discussions. Panelists may be asked to judge many proposals in a short, intense time period, but you can make your work stand out by providing concise, precise, memorable sentences and phrases in the project summary or goals section. Remember that whatever you write in the summary will be used to highlight major aspects of your study, so be sure to state exactly what you mean.

There is no template for designing an effective project summary. Some of the most compelling summaries start with a broad statement of purpose and then funnel the reader to the specifics of the proposed work (see Chapter 3). Nor is there a template for producing a summary. Some authors write the summary and then use it as an outline for the grant application; others write it after the rest of the proposal is completed. The essential feature is that the summary accurately reflect the project. Summaries from several

funded proposals appear below (with the permission of
their authors). You may wish to critique these before
writing your own project summary.

Elements of an Effective
Project Summary

Our discussion centers on a model for NSF basic research proposals in which the initial section is
termed Project Summary. For NIH proposals this section is labeled Specific Aims (Reif-Lehrer 1995); every
agency may have a different title or slightly different
format for the precise part of the document where the
proposed research is summarized. However, the goals
of these sections are generally similar. Before writing
this element, be sure to obtain precise specifications.

The NSF's description of the Project Summary
reads: "[The summary] should not be an abstract of the
proposal, but rather a self-contained description of the
activity that would result if the proposal were
funded. . . . [It] should include a statement of objectives, methods to be employed and the significance of
the proposed activity. . . . [I]nsofar as possible, [it
should be] understandable to a scientifically or techni-
cally literate lay reader."

This general statement distinguishes a proposal summary from a manuscript abstract. In a proposal for a basic research project, you report what you plan to do and stress why your work will be influential, not what you have done and why it is important. Emphasis is placed on significance and context, and it is essential to establish that there will be consequential outputs. For a task-oriented proposal you highlight the expected outputs and the novel aspects or particular qualifications that justify your selection over others for the specified goals. Results are not included in a summary, although you may refer to your previous research to make a point or to establish your ability to accomplish the proposed task. Length limits for summaries vary with the funding agency, but they rarely exceed a single-spaced page. Although agencies expect scientists to write the summary in a way that can be understood by a scientifically literate lay audience, this can be difficult for some writers.

Before you begin to write your summary, be aware of the conventions in your field (e.g., are hypotheses or objectives presented in the summary?). Ask friends and colleagues for copies of summaries they have written, and read or download summaries or abstracts of funded proposals (they are in the public domain) at the Web sites of major funding agencies; see also the examples below.

The two-paragraph project summary model. In your summary you have just a few sentences in which to direct the reader from the most general and broad significance of your proposed research to its specific details. A number of styles and formats can be successful. Some summaries begin with a bold statement: "The proposed work will test the hypothesis that . . ." Others employ a more gradual development of ideas or build chronologically from early views to the current state of the field. The second style is logical, but it may fail to capture the reader's interest at the start. We encourage you to start by writing a two-paragraph summary. Use the first paragraph to introduce the problem and describe the work, and the second paragraph to emphasize the potential outcome and significance.

Paragraph 1

- Develop the broadest context for the research in the first one or two sentences.

- State your research questions as testable hypotheses or, where appropriate, as objectives. Never propose untestable hypotheses, or goals that can not be met with the proposed research.

- Identify gaps in current knowledge and state how your questions fill those gaps or lead the field forward. Establish the overall importance or relevance of your work. This tactic will also help to justify funding your study relative to other well-conceived studies.

• If appropriate, include preliminary results of your own work; these make further work compelling and establish your credibility.

• In the last few sentences of the paragraph, give a detailed, succinct description of the actual work that you will do.

Paragraph 2

• Briefly summarize or describe techniques, study sites, and, if appropriate, the taxonomic names of study organisms (this may be in the first or second paragraph).

• Discuss the projected results or output from your proposed study.

• State how your work will advance your area of study; perhaps include a phrase or sentence on the implications of your work for other fields or issues. Be careful about making statements that cannot be supported by your work.

The following project summary illustrates some of these ideas: it uses the two-paragraph model, and it

provides a context for the study. There are testable hypotheses stated clearly, and the broader value of the
study is stressed.

Role of Winter Water Relations in Determining the Upper Elevational Limits of Three New England Conifers

Winter desiccation is recognized as an important stress factor in coniferous forests, and it may limit conifer distribution. Most research to date has focused on desiccation at alpine treeline, whereas little attention has been given to its role in establishing the upper elevational limit of low-elevation conifers. Our objective is to test the hypothesis that winter water relations limit the upper elevational range of low-elevation evergreen conifers in New England. This will be the first study to examine desiccation stress in non-subalpine conifers. The winter water relations of three low-elevation conifers will be examined: white pine (*Pinus strobus* L.), eastern hemlock (*Tsuga canadensis* [L.] Carr.), and red pine (*P. resinosa* Ait.). Each of these three species differs in its habitat preference and growth strategy. Preliminary results indicate that older foliage in each species can reach water levels expected to cause desiccation damage. Our approach will use physiological measurements of trees (relative water content, water potential, and cuticular resistance) collected near the upper elevational limit of each species during the winter to assess desiccation stress. These data, along with micrometeorological data collected at field sites, will be used to predict winter water relations. We will test the following hypotheses: (1) water levels in foliage near the upper elevational distribution of each species will approach or fall below lethal desiccation levels; and (2) cuticular resistance will decrease over the course of the winter. Even if this work does not support these hypotheses, the understanding of conifer responses to winter climate will be greatly increased.

This study will be of value to plant stress physiologists and plant ecologists. It is unique in that it will combine field assessments of desiccation with micrometeorological measurements in a model, allowing plant water relations to be explicitly coupled to climate. Such an approach sets the stage for future studies of limitations by winter desiccation, using other species and under conditions imposed by a changing climate.

Source: R. L. Boyce and A. J. Friedland

Examples of abstracts on the Web. While writing this chapter we read more than a hundred project summaries from grant applications for projects that were funded by U.S. agencies. The summaries were from a variety of fields represented in this book (e.g., environmental science, ecology, molecular biology, earth sciences, atmospheric sciences, and neuro- biology) and available on the Internet or through published annual reports of major funding agencies. We focused mainly on summaries from NSF and U.S. Department of Agriculture. Summaries from these proposals varied greatly, yet we found many similari- ties, which we incorporated into the suggestions pre- sented in this chapter. For example, all explain the sig- nificance of their research topic and specify their research questions. By reading these summaries and others (see the list of Web addresses at the end of this chapter) you will decide which styles and approaches you prefer.

Here is another summary that combines many of the important features. This author uses three paragraphs rather than two.

Modeling Anthropogenic Desiccation of the Aral Sea: A Unique Test of the Predictive Capabilities of a Regional Earth System Model

The utility of global and regional earth system models (ESMs) for causes of past climate change, and for predicting impacts of human activities, depends on how accurately changes driven by perturbations are predicted. This accuracy is controlled by how well feedbacks are simulated. The accuracy of model-predicted changes is unknown, because previous model validation has been limited to assessing how well present conditions are reproduced, or to comparing paleoclimate model results with sparse and potentially ambiguous proxy data. In order to conduct a more thorough evaluation of ESM performance, model-predicted and observed changes resulting from known perturbations over historical timescales will be compared.

In this study, anthropogenic desiccation of the Aral Sea will be used as a test of the predictive accuracy of a regional ESM (the RegCM2 and lake model associated with the National Center for Atmospheric Research) that includes an interactively coupled atmosphere and lake. Desiccation of the Aral Sea since 1960, resulting from diversion of water for intensive irrigation in the surrounding basin, has been extensive enough to produce a regional climatic response. Desiccation of this magnitude should also produce a model response. Importantly, meteorological and hydrologic observations that span the interval of desiccation are available, so the actual changes can be quantified. The predictive capabilities of the model will be tested by comparing model-simulated changes with observed changes that have occurred between 1960 and 1995.

The work consists of three components. First, it will be used to quantify regional climate and lake hydrologic changes that are likely due to Aral Sea desiccation. These observed changes will be used to (i) test model predictions, (ii) directly measure how the presence of the Aral Sea alters regional climate, (iii) directly measure how lake-level variations have impacted the Aral Sea's hydrology, and (iv) quantify regional-scale human impacts. Second, the interactively coupled RegCM2-lake model's strengths in predicting changes will be assessed by comparing simulated and observed desiccation-induced regional climate and lake hydrologic changes. In order to gain a more thorough understanding of the causes for the coupled model's successes and failures, the predictive accuracy of independent (non-interactive) versions of RegCM2 and the lake model, driven by meteorological or hydrologic observations, will also be evaluated. Third, the regional climate effects generated by the Aral for seas of different surface area, depth, and salinity will be calculated. This will allow:
(i) quantification of lake-atmosphere interactions and feedbacks associated with lake-level variations;
(ii) prediction of future climate changes driven by further anthropogenic Aral Sea desiccation; and
(iii) assessment of how much of the model predicted change between pre-desiccation and present

intervals was due to large-scale meteorological variability. Predictions of future climate changes resulting from additional desiccation will be prepared and evaluated in terms of the model's strengths and weaknesses as determined. This research is important because it seeks to test how well coupled regional climate lake models predict the impact of human activities on a large shallow terminal lake and how that feedbacks on the regional and global climate.

Source: L. C. Sloan

This summary has a number of strengths: it presents the overarching questions that justify the study, identifies gaps in the current knowledge to be filled by this research, describes the work to be done (without excessive detail), and states what the author feels will be the significant outputs. It does not include a series of testable hypotheses, but it is not essential that all project summaries do this (and the need for this varies among disciplines).

Exercises for Writing a Project Summary

Before you write your own project summary, read and critique a number of others. For example, modify a few sentences in our previous sample summaries (Chapter 5) to see whether you can improve them. Try adding hypotheses or working with the placement of the significance statements. Ask yourself, Is the writing easily understood by the reader? Does it flow from topic to topic? Are transitions smooth and clear? Read the summary out loud to see.

Critiquing other summaries. We have constructed two versions of a project summary. See whether you can improve on each version. Make comments directly on the summary, or photocopy the text and make comments on the copy.

Version 1
Effects of Nutrient Additions on Red Spruce Health and Nutrition

The purpose of the proposed study is to determine the effects of nutrient additions on carbon fixation and foliar nutrition of high-elevation red spruce in the northeastern United States. Trees in this ecosystem are declining, a circumstance that has been attributed in part to a changing chemical environment. Earlier work has shown that nitrogen and sulfur inputs are quite high, and nitrogen saturation has been suggested as a cause of decline. Work from the southern Appalachians suggests that acidic deposition–induced calcium deficiency, perhaps coupled with aluminum mobilization, causes increased rates of respiration and reduced photosynthesis: respiration ratios which lead to reduced growth. Work with potted spruce seedlings from the South has confirmed this, and it is consistent with patterns observed in the field. Preliminary data by our group suggest that in New Hampshire, 1) spruce respond positively to additions of nitrogen, and 2) there are adequate supplies of base cations. Data from New York suggest that 1) nitrogen additions reduce foliar growth, and 2) calcium is limiting. We recognize that some of these findings are, in part, inconsistent with previous findings, and thus we wish to extend our investigations.

We propose to conduct a field study using naturally grown spruce saplings on Mount Jefferson (White Mountains, New Hampshire, United States) and Mount Marcy (Adirondacks, New York, United States). Fertilizer treatments using N, Ca, and/or Mg will be applied over the three-year course of the study. Photosynthesis and dark respiration will be measured throughout the growing season to determine the response to different treatments. Foliar concentrations and contents of N, base cations, and Al will be analyzed to determine their effects on carbon fixation rates.

This study will increase our understanding of the impact of global changes in atmospheric chemistry on high-elevation red spruce–balsam fir forests. However, our research has potential significance beyond this particular ecosystem, for it will show how conifers in general respond to abiotic stress. Chronic levels of stress, such as those induced by global change, often initiate forest declines. The early stages of decline are often subtle and therefore overlooked, creating difficulty in identifying the onset of decline. The research proposed here will make use of a species that is known to be in decline, across a gradient from low to high levels of decline.

Source: A. J. Friedland

Version 2
Effects of Nutrient Additions on Red Spruce Health and Nutrition

Nutrient deficiencies and imbalances are known to cause problems in plant growth and metabolism. High levels of nitrogen and sulfur deposition in the northeastern United States are suspected of causing nutrient imbalances at higher elevations. Many hypotheses related to N, S, Ca, and Al have been offered to explain the decline of red spruce at high elevations in the Northeast. Preliminary data by our group suggest that in New Hampshire, 1) spruce respond positively to additions of N, and 2) there are adequate supplies of base cations. Others have suggested that Ca supplies may be limiting. We propose to conduct a field study using naturally grown spruce saplings on Mount Jefferson in the White Mountains of New Hampshire. Fertilizer treatments of N, Ca, and/or Mg will be applied over the three-year course of the study. Photosynthesis and dark respiration will be measured throughout the growing season to determine the response to different treatments. Foliar concentrations and contents of N, base cations, and Al will be analyzed to determine their effects on carbon fixation rates.

This study will increase our understanding of the impact of atmospheric deposition of pollutants on high-elevation red spruce–balsam fir forests, and it may provide information on how conifers in general respond to abiotic stress. Chronic levels of stress can initiate forest declines in other temperate coniferous forests.

Source: A. J. Friedland

We feel that the first version could be substantially improved. For example, findings are reported in a chronological or sequential order. "Work from . . . ," "Work with . . ." constructions become repetitive and are not the most integrative and synthetic way to present information. The questions and hypotheses are not explicitly stated. Do you feel that the potential significance of the work is clearly stated? One way to amend this abstract would be to delete most of the first paragraph, describe the general area of nutrient deficiencies first, and identify the unanswered questions more succinctly. The second version is better but still fails to articulate hypotheses.

Here are some other summaries from successful grants that we downloaded from agency Web pages (used with permission of the authors). All are quite forceful, but even the best summaries can be improved. Try to enrich each one.

Mathematical Models of the Cell Division Cycle

The cell division cycle is the periodic repetition of certain events—DNA synthesis, mitosis, and cytokinesis—that transform a single cell into two daughter cells. Cell division must be coordinated to overall cell growth; otherwise, cells could become arbitrarily large or vanishingly small. By observing how cells respond to perturbations of the division cycle, cell biologists discovered that the DNA-to-protein ratio plays an essential role in determining the timing of mitosis and cell division. Recently, molecular studies have revealed four classes of proteins that participate prominently in the division control mechanism. Two proteins (cdc2 and cyclin) combine to form a heterodimer ("mitosis promoting factor," or MPF) that, when activated, triggers all the major events of mitosis and cell division. The activity of MPF is, in turn, controlled by protein kinases and protein phosphatases that determine the phosphorylation state of MPF. The long-range goal of this research is to develop mathematical models of the cell division cycle in order to build secure, reliable connections between hard-won molecular details of the control mechanisms and classical observations of the behavior of the intact regulatory system. The model will describe the regulation of MPF activity by phosphorylation, and how the phosphorylation state of MPF is determined by the DNA-to-protein ratio of the cell. The mathematical approach is a tool to refine our assumptions and guide our reasoning about the essential events of cell growth and division.

The goal of this research is to develop mathematical models of the cell division cycle. The mathematical modeling will be based on recent evidence concerning the biochemical control mechanisms involved in this fundamental life process. The mathematical models will be useful in further refining the interpretations of experimental data and as a guide in planning future experiments that ultimately should lead to a thorough understanding of how the cell division cycle is regulated.

Source: J. J. Tyson

Biochemistry of Fatty Acid Transport in Escherichia coli

In all organisms, fatty acids (FA) and their derivatives are components of membranes, are sources of metabolic energy, and are effector molecules that regulate metabolism. This research is on the transport of long-chain fatty acids (C14-C18) into the cell, followed by their enzymatic conversion to coenzyme A thioesters prior to metabolism. These FAs traverse the cell envelope of *Escherichia coli* by a specific, energy-dependent process that requires the outer membrane-bound FA binding protein FadL and the inner membrane associated acyl CoA synthetase (ACS). ACS activates FAs concomitant with transport and results in net FA accumulation in the cell against a concentration gradient. Processes that govern FadL-mediated long-chain FA transport across the outer membrane will be determined by i) evaluating the topology of FadL using limited proteolysis and protein modification and ii) defining the FA binding pocket within FadL using the affinity labeled long-chain fatty acid 9-p-azidophenoxy nonanoic acid (3H-APNA). The contribution of acyl CoA synthetase to long-chain FA transport will be evaluated by i) defining the ATP and FA binding domains within ACS using the affinity labeled ligands azido- (32P ATP and 3H-APNA, respectively), and ii) mutagenesis of the FadL gene at specific sites involved in CoA and/or FA binding. Studies are also being conducted to define protein-protein interactions between the membrane-bound (FadL) and soluble protein components of this transport system using Far Western analyses, and by performing experiments with glutathione S-transferase (GST) and histidine fusion proteins. Soluble protein components may interact with FadL. The H+/FA cotransporter in the inner cell membrane, and acyl CoA dehydrogenase and acyl CoA binding protein in the cell cytosol may bind specifically with ACS.

Source: P. N. Black

Theory and Experiments on the Function of Visual Cortex

This project will be supported under the NSF program on Integrating Enabling Technologies into Neuroscience Research; it is a collaboration of mathematicians and neuroscientists attacking the most important issues in brain research. In our view, the premier problem facing us is how to understand the function of the cerebral cortex of the brain as a functioning neural network. We study the part of the cerebral cortex that handles visual information— called the visual cortex. Cells in the visual cortex are selectively sensitive for the orientations of the visual boundaries of objects. We will develop and test neural network models for this selectivity, to see whether it is a property that emerges from interactions between nerve cells in the cerebral cortex, or whether it is a passive by-product of the connections to cortical cells from lower levels of the visual system of the brain. We believe that understanding the neural basis for orientation tuning in the visual cortex may be crucial for understanding the function of the entire cortex. If we find evidence that interaction between neighboring neurons in the cerebral cortex is essential for orientation tuning to work, then this will be crucial support for the idea that the cerebral cortex is a richly interconnected, interactive neural network that can be studied with available analytical tools.

Source: D. W. McLaughlin and R. Shapley

Search the Web. The following Web addresses, accurate as of press time, provide access to summaries of funded grants from federal agencies. These sites also provide much more information about suggestions and requirements regarding proposals (other Web sites are listed in appendix 2):

- National Science Foundation:
  http://www.nsf.gov/

- USDA National Research Initiative Competitive Grants Program:
  http://www.reeusda.gov/nri/

- Environmental Protection Agency:
  http://www.epa.gov/docs/ord/

- National Institutes of Health:
  http://www.nih.gov/

Objectives and Hypotheses: An Exhaustive List Is Exhausting

A beautifully crafted document, or a convincing and exciting significance statement, means little if the research objectives and tests are ill conceived, poorly stated, or absent. Our class concentrates heavily on constructing, deconstructing, and reconstructing each others' objectives and hypotheses. If working alone, you might want to find a few colleagues who are willing to exchange ideas. Reviewing your hypotheses and objectives with others may be one of the most beneficial activities you can pursue.

Development of hypotheses generally precedes proposal writing. Most readers of this book probably have already identified a series of objectives and associated hypotheses. Solicit feedback prior to writing by presenting these hypotheses to colleagues and mentors to determine whether they are rigorous, testable, and engaging. The goal now is to articulate those ideas in writing and to place them into a proposal. A key aspect of this process is making sure that the hypotheses are consistent with the significance statement and linked properly to the objectives.

Objectives versus Hypotheses

Objectives usually refer to broad, scientifically far-reaching aspects of a study, and sometimes they verge on significance statements. If both significance statements and objectives are included, the objectives generally are more focused. Objectives can also pertain primarily to contributions or novel uses of the data within the scientific community. We label these objective statements Type 1 and Type 2. The following examples are modified from proposals that we have written or that have been shared with us by the authors.

> Our objectives are:
>
> - to further our understanding of the implications of global climate change in freshwater lake plankton communities. (Type 1)
> - to lead to more informed policy decisions about the effect of electromagnetic radiation on humans residing near high-voltage power lines. (Type 2)

- to understand how cell division and differentiation are regulated by a myriad of extracellular and intracellular signals. (Type 1)
- to evaluate mechanisms leading to species coexistence in marine intertidal communities and compare magnitudes and scales of effects. (Type 1)
- to provide the first complete data base for the assessment of toxic metals on reproduction. (Type 2)
- to develop an analytical framework for classifying brain potential analysis of motor function and decisions. (Type 1)

Hypotheses usually refer to an even more specific set of testable conjectures than do the objectives. A well-formulated hypothesis leads directly to the experiments and sampling programs that form the basis for the research. Keep the number of hypotheses reasonable: it is important to strike the proper balance between too many and too few. If you present too many, your proposal will confuse the reader and reduce its effectiveness. One of us wrote a proposal with twenty-seven hypotheses. Rather than being dazzled with the breadth and depth of thinking and synthesis involved in the study, the reviewers were baffled and bored. They also perceived a lack of focus—no surprise! After the proposal was rejected, the program director suggested reducing the number of hypotheses to five or fewer to focus the effort. We agree with that general recommendation, though there is no magic number for how many hypotheses to include.

We have adapted some hypotheses from our own and others' proposals. Is it apparent how these hypotheses differ from general significance statements or objectives?

- We hypothesize that lead is complexed by a chelating agent associated with adventitious roots, transported across the membrane, and stored in the inner cortex.
- Channel roughness is greater, and velocity, stream power, and shear stress are lower, in restored reaches versus unrestored reaches.
- Differences in temperature and humidity among sites persist across years, despite natural yearly variation in climate and other environmental variation.
- Zinc can effectively compete with other metals for enzyme-active sites, transporter proteins, and other biologically important ligands.
- Mineral weathering in the lower soil horizons provides most of the cations lost from the ecosystem to stream water.

Linking Objectives and Hypotheses to the Significance

Although objectives, hypotheses, and overall significance refer to different key features of a research proposal, they are tightly linked and must work well to-

gether. Each relies on the other for its validity and purpose. The significance statement is the most general
and far-reaching description of the research; objectives
are usually more focused than is the significance, and
hypotheses are more specific than are the objectives.
Objectives and hypotheses are more likely to identify
particular processes, organisms, or locations than are
significance statements.

To illustrate the relation between significance,
objective, and hypothesis, we return to an example
from Chapter 4 (from F. M. M. Morel). In this example,
the overall *significance* statement introduces the topic of
metal pollution and its major effects on agriculture as
the overall focus of the study:

> Understanding how metal pollutants affect crops
> and forests is obviously of great importance to U.S.
> agriculture.

One of the *objectives* in that same proposal identifies
the metal pollution of interest as coming from smelters
and being airborne:

> [We wish to determine whether] in areas of high
> metal pollution, such as those near smelters, are
> plants exposed to metal stress through direct
> airborne pollution or [indirectly] through
> accumulation in soils?

Later on, the author presents this *hypothesis*, which
names the metals as Ni and Cu, the mechanism as at-

mospheric deposition, and the focal plant species as
paper birch:

> To investigate the hypothesis that current
> atmospheric deposition of nickel and copper aerosols
> is the dominant source of metal stress in vegetation
> surrounding Sudbury, Ontario, seedling of *Betula*
> *papyrifera* will be placed at each sampling location.

Note how the author becomes increasingly specific in
the move from significance to objectives to hypotheses,
and how each is closely linked to the others.

Here is another illustration of the progression.
The *significance* statement is broad in scope and relates
to a problem of international concern, namely global
climate change. In creating this example we deliber-
ately avoided the popular terminology, but that is a
matter of personal preference:

> We wish to understand the biological implications of
> projected increases in global temperature on fish
> populations.

The *objective* is much more precise and is directed to a
particular type of system (salmonids on the rearing
grounds), yet it remains somewhat inclusive (not re-
gionally focused, nor species specific):

> We will quantify responses of salmon to predicted
> increases in summer temperatures in their rearing
> grounds.

Finally, the two *hypotheses* that derive from this objective lead directly to an easily identifiable set of experiments or measurements. They are species-specific and address certain demographic traits and rates:

> A water temperature increase of 1°C in May will advance the hatching date of Atlantic salmon by 2 weeks.
>
> Advancing the hatching date of Atlantic salmon by 2 weeks will reduce survival rates.

In this example we also have become increasingly specific, moving from significance to objectives to hypotheses.

Placement in the Proposal

Successful proposals often feature significance, objectives, and hypotheses sections near the start of the proposal, but there is no specified location for them. Authors usually introduce objectives and even hypotheses in the project summary or aims, and the objectives almost always appear in the significance section of proposals. You need to strike a balance between early presentation and appearing repetitious when you discuss the same material in greater detail in later sections. Many authors insert the hypotheses in a number of locations in a proposal, presenting greater detail with each mention.

In the following example, the general hypothesis is first stated in the title and then repeated with greater detail, and in a different fashion, in various sections of the proposal:

- *Title.* "The Role of Temporal Control Genes in Specifying the Timing of Events in the Nematode *C. elegans*"

- *Project summary.* "The broad goal of this work is to understand the genetic and molecular mechanisms of the temporal control of cell division and differentiation using the nematode *C. elegans* as a model.

- *Introduction and background.* "Animal development is a complex schedule of processes that are controlled by genetic and other factors."

- *Significance section.* "The *C. elegans* genes offer an opportunity to study the genetic and molecular mechanisms controlling cell division and differentiation, processes central to all multicellular development."

- *Research design and methods.* The hypotheses are presented in a preface to each set of experiments which are designed to test them.
  Source: V. Ambros

Regardless of where you cite your objectives and hypotheses, and depending on the requirements of your funding agency or dissertation committee, using headings and subheadings highlights the importance of objectives and hypotheses within the proposal. It also makes it easier for the reviewers to find them. Be sure to follow the conventions of your field. For example, the practice in some fields is to use the traditional null hypothesis; that is, no matter what you think the outcome of your study might be, you state that there will be no effect (e.g., "The test drug will have no effect on the population."). Other fields are more accepting of positive hypotheses ("The test drug will reduce symptoms in more than 75 percent of the test population."). The terminology used may also vary across disciplines (e.g., hypotheses are sometimes referred to as questions).

Exercises for Writing Objectives and Hypotheses

Our class uses the following exercise to formulate a very tight set of hypotheses prior to writing the accompanying text. This formulation step may take several weeks as you review the critical feedback on your objectives and hypotheses and then revise and restate. This exercise is a strong follow-up to exercises 1 through 4 in Chapter 4.

EXERCISE 5. Prepare a ten- to fifteen-minute presentation of the objectives and hypotheses of your study, focusing on the direct links between them. As in the previous exercises, justify the importance of your hypotheses with respect to the larger field of theoretical and empirical research preceding it. Hypotheses must be concise and easily understood, and the flow among the hypotheses must be logical. If you are writing this exercise, confine the text to fewer than two pages. Work to develop a sensible progression and transition among ideas.

We again urge you to collect as many proposals as possible and to evaluate them on your own or with a group. In addition to considering logic and flow, also assess the style of presentation. One widespread problem we see is that some authors number their objectives or hypotheses in a confusing manner (e.g., "I.A.b.iii"), which can diminish the strength of the final work. This is a minor point, but as we've noted elsewhere, a clear presentation of objectives and hypotheses is extremely important.

Lay the Foundation in the Introduction

Once you provide reviewers or your committee members with a perspective on the significance of your research and steer them toward your objectives, your work begins in earnest. You now need to create the essential elements of what NSF terms "The Project Description" and NIH calls "The Research Plan."

The introduction or background is a major element of the project description or research plan. In this section, you should review the literature and stress key references. You may choose to introduce relevant conceptual, theoretical, or empirical models, or to discuss the need for new methods or technologies if they are pivotal to your research. To set the stage for your proposed study and to establish your ability to accomplish the task, a summary of your own relevant prior re-

search or preliminary results is also often included
here or even in a separate section. The main goal of the
introduction is to lead the reviewer to your objectives,
hypotheses, and proposed research based on an
overview of current research.

> Suggested Order of Presentation of the Project
> Description
> III. Project description (following from Chapter 3)
>   A. Results from prior agency support (this
>   chapter)
>   B. Statement of the problem and significance
>   (Chapter 4)
>   C. Introduction and background (this chapter)
>   • Relevant literature review (this chapter)
>   • Preliminary data (this chapter)
>   • Conceptual, empirical, or theoretical model
>   (this chapter)
>   • Justification of approach or novel methods
>   (this chapter)

The introduction must funnel the reader from
a general review of the literature to your specific
study. After reading a persuasive introduction, the
reader should exclaim, "Of course! What a great idea
for a research project. Why didn't I think of that?" The
introduction section provides an excellent opportunity to establish why your work is compelling and to
capture the attention of a committee or funding
agency.

The Basics of Introductions

Results from prior agency support. An introduction may begin with a section for prior results, which generally refers to either 1) results of research that was previously funded by the agency to which the current proposal is being submitted, or 2) your own preliminary data that are essential to the proposed work. This type of information may not be needed in most gradate dissertation proposals, where preliminary results may be more effectively blended directly into the introduction–background section. However, if you or any of your co-investigators have prior research that has been funded by the agency to which you are applying, you may be required to summarize your results in a specific section. NSF and some other agencies require a feature called "Results from Prior Agency Support." Typically this appears as the first part of the project description, preceding even the significance statement.

Reviewers of proposals are always asked to comment on an applicant's productivity and on the quality of his or her previous work, so this section may have an important influence on whether a project is funded. Keep your prior research statement concise, citing your published work where appropriate. We advise using this section to prove your past success and productivity and highlight previous results that have been insightful and that lay the groundwork for the new research. Seek guidance from the program director at your agency for specifics on the types and amount of information typically contained in this section. Remember that for most proposals, space is at a premium. Allotting too much text to this part of the proposal will naturally restrict the space that can be used to present other material. Avoid providing information that will distract from the proposal at hand.

Even if it is not required, a prior results section is reasonable if the current proposal is an extension or continuation of previously funded work, or if a result or discovery from the prior work is relevant to the proposed work. If your prior work is not related to the proposed work but a statement is still required, keep the mention short and consider putting it at the end of the project description, where it is less likely to draw attention away from the current proposal.

Preliminary results. If you are a beginning researcher or are new to a particular field, you will probably not have results from previous related work. However, even new researchers may have generated preliminary data that should be included in the proposal. A prior or preliminary results section within the introduction may be an appropriate location for your own unpublished, preparatory data. By placing your preliminary results here you can establish your competency or the likely success or novelty of your proposed research. Avoid overstating the implications of your results, and avoid concentrating on them to the detriment of making the case for your new project.

Provide a Strong Foundation for Your Research in the Body of the Introduction

As in the introduction to a manuscript, you must cover the key concepts, previous work, and important publications that will allow an informed scientist from another field to understand the *motivation* for your research. At the same time, this section should not be too elementary for experts in the field. To paraphrase Robert Day (1988) in his book on writing scientific papers: An ideal proposal introduction allows the reader to understand and evaluate the proposed work without needing to refer to previous publications on the topic.

There is no one right way to organize your introduction, but we continue to suggest funneling from the general to the specific. Some authors build from the specific to the general, however. Try articulating your own arguments in each of these ways to see which allows you to be the most concise, logical, and interesting.

References in the Proposal

Remember that throughout the proposal you must make a case for the importance of your research; in the introduction you can reinforce the relevance and need for the study. Use current and widely accepted references wherever possible to support your arguments and to channel the reader to your specific research objectives.

There is much uncertainty about the use of references in research proposals. Here are a few common questions (see also Chapter 12):

• How many references should I include?

• Which ones?

• Will references to hypotheses that compete with my work diminish my arguments?

- Should I use controversial papers?

- Do I need to justify my methods using the literature?

One of the first questions we hear concerns how many references to include. The issue is the quality rather than the quantity of references. It is vital to illustrate or support your major points with important references, but you do not need to include ten papers illustrating each item that you raise. Include the references that have guided the development of the field, and be sure to include any new references that are germane to your arguments.

The literature review must be considered thorough. Proposals are often criticized for not including "key" references, which we take to mean the most widely accepted or influential papers on a topic. And if you are trying to establish that there is a gap in the literature in an area, you must be especially careful with your literature review—you would not want to say there were no published papers on a topic only to have reviewers point out references that you missed. Another critical component of being thorough is the incorporation not only of references that support your contentions but also of those that conflict with your arguments or are difficult to resolve with respect to those

arguments. New authors frequently ignore this aspect
of proposal writing. Yet many reviewers make a point
of considering both sides of all arguments, so this
omission can be fatal to a proposal. Being thorough
may also require that you cite controversial material. If
you do so, be certain that you understand the reasons
for its controversy in the field. Take special care if such
papers provide the critical justification for your research (i.e., if you use them as a foundation for your
own study).

Ask yourself if each concept or paper is worth
citing. Bear in mind that you have limited space in
which to develop your topic. Avoid unnecessary detail,
parenthetical issues, and topics not specifically related
to the proposal; they can be distracting, and they may
suggest to reviewers that you have not clearly identified
the key concepts and issues related to your proposal.
We have even read introductions that endeavor to provide background on all aspects of a topic *except* the one
the investigator plans to study! Imagine a proposal on
the effects of climate change on soil microbial decomposition. If the author were to begin the background
section by reviewing climate change theory, changes in
greenhouse gases over time, and the evidence for and
against global warming, it would be difficult to guess
where the proposal was leading. There would not be an

effective funnel, key arguments would not have been highlighted, and the reader could be well into the proposal before the relation between climate change, soil moisture, and soil microbial decomposition was established.

The Role of Models

The authors of some of the strongest proposals use conceptual, graphical, synthetic, theoretical, and analytical models to frame their research questions and design. Models, standard practice in some fields and less common in others, can be far more effective than words. Models are usually presented in the introduction and background sections and are often represented in the text with tables, figures, or sets of equations. It should be clear to the reader whether a model being used is your own or adapted from the literature. During the formulation of their research proposals, many scientists develop conceptual or analytical models that they publish as free-standing works.

Models have many different formats. Conceptual models are commonly used to identify the components of a study or the processes leading to and deriving from a central theme. A "box model"—a set of boxes and arrows that shows how your research question fits into a larger picture—may be effective.

Empirical models or calculations are also useful for synthesizing introductory and conceptual material. Many successful investigators apply a computer simulation or a few simple calculations to data from their own work or the literature in order to generate new figures, diagrams, or synthesized data that provide motivation and perspective for the current research. This is particularly effective when you do not have preliminary data but want to demonstrate that your ideas are feasible. The need to provide details about the model (e.g., specific equations, parameter sources, constants, hierarchical organization) depends on how fully the model predictions form the basis of your proposed research. However, you must ensure that you do not raise more questions than you answer by including the model. We urge you to ask colleagues who have used models to provide critical feedback on this topic.

Quantitative models can also be used to generate analytical solutions or predictions resulting from more formal mathematical expressions of conceptual or qualitative models. However, avoid models so complicated or untested that they are better suited to publish first in a peer-reviewed publication. The introduction is one potential location for a quantitative model;

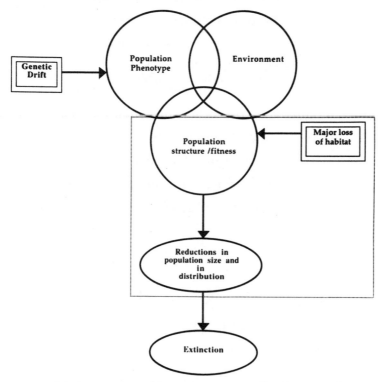

A model showing possible consequences of anthropogenic habitat loss on population structure and fitness, distribution, and extinction. In this example, the dotted lines indicate the area that the hypothetical proposal will examine. Modified from Gilpin and Soulé (1986).

the methods section is another (Chapter 9). If the
thrust of your proposal is modeling, then obviously you
must present most of the details, probably in the methods section or in a section devoted to the model. If your
model is a tool used to interpret or apply results, however, it is probably sufficient to present a short paragraph describing it, along with a few references to
more detailed descriptions of how it is used. If you
have modified a model from the literature but have not
published your modifications, you should describe, if
not show, your changes.

Are Objectives and Hypotheses Part of the Introduction?

It is common for the introductory section to
conclude with a list and brief discussion of the objectives and hypotheses. These should derive easily from
the background material preceding them. Some people
prefer to include them in the research plan (Chapter 9)
or as a separate element of the proposal; in either case,
they must mesh logically with material in the introduction.

In some instances, it is necessary to provide literature support for the employment of a particular ap-

proach or method, or for the use of a special type of instrumentation. If these are controversial or novel, the literature and preliminary results that endorse your project should be featured in the introduction and background. Your evidence for the successful use of these approaches will be of special interest to reviewers, who need to assess the feasibility as well as the importance of the proposed research.

Crafting the Introduction

We emphasize three issues when writing and organizing the introductory sections:

- Focus on the important points and establish their relevance to your proposal.

- Do not make this section too long.

- Use schematics, models, headings, and formatting to channel the reader and to show the direction the proposal is taking.

Introductory sections often are too long. A length of three to four single-spaced pages is common. Remember, this would be nearly 25 percent of an NSF-type fifteen-page proposal. To take advantage of this limited space, you must choose your material wisely so as not to dilute your message. Organize your points strategically to channel the reader to your research, and break up text with headings, figures, and tables. Explain to the reader why you are presenting specific details by providing section and subsection headings, topic sentences, transitions, and written road maps such as, "In the following section we develop a framework for . . ."

Parts of the background may be nicely summarized with a figure or table. Figures are impressive if you have made them yourself and if they synthesize a number of different papers culled from the literature. Reviewers usually prefer to examine a figure or table embedded in the text rather than read two or three paragraphs of prose.

Exercises for Writing the Introduction and Background

It is difficult to isolate exercises specific to writing the background or introduction of a research proposal. As usual, reading and critiquing other proposals and having others evaluate your own are the best preparation. It may be useful to consider good review papers as templates for an effective background. A strong synthetic review usually brings together the literature to support a set of central conjectures or to reveal a vital gap in knowledge. In this way it is similar to a proposal background.

The exercises that we presented in Chapter 4 lead to the development of the conceptual framework, the project summary, and underlying qualitative or quantitative models. These drills all require you to frame your questions within the context of the existing literature or of your own preliminary results, so they are also preparation for drafting this section. In particular, exercise 3 promotes the construction of a model or series of models to identify the key relations between processes that form the basis for a model in your introduction.

Finally, it is usually instructive to summarize the elements of your research design schematically. Try constructing several diagrams or figures that could help you formulate a verbal description of your research plan. If this method proves effective, you may choose to use this to help frame the introduction for your project. If your introduction is a success, the reader will be eager to reflect on the research plan that you have devised to test your hypotheses and meet your objectives.

Experimental Design and Methods: What Will You Actually Do?

The introduction and background should provide sufficient material to give the reader a solid appreciation of the importance of your proposed objectives and hypotheses. The next big step is to craft the unit referred to by NSF as the Research Plan. This element contains the nitty-gritty of the implementation, analysis, and interpretation of your study. This is where you convince the reader that your project can be accomplished.

Suggested Order of Presentation of the Research Plan

III. Project description (following from Chapter 3)
  A. Results from prior agency support (Chapter 8)
  B. Statement of the problem and significance Chapter 4)
  C. Introduction and background (Chapter 8)
    • Relevant literature review
    • Preliminary data

- Conceptual or empirical model
- Justification of approach or novel methods
D. Research plan (this chapter)
  - Overview of research design
  - Objectives, hypotheses, and methods
  - Analysis and expected results (see also Chapter 10)
  - Timetable (Chapter 11)

The research plan is usually broken down into a number of separate elements. In this chapter we cover the parts that deal with research strategy and methods. The trick is to keep from getting bogged down in detail. You must ask yourself, "Too much, too little, or just enough?" in writing this section of your proposal. There are several crucial questions that will be asked by thoughtful reviewers as they assess your design, methods, and analysis sections:

- Are these the correct and best methods for the specific questions?

- Are the methods proven and properly cited?

- Are the methods feasible given the time and support available?

- Is the precision or extent of the study appropriate and sufficient to answer questions, hypotheses or objectives?

- Are the investigators competent in the use of all these techniques?

- What critical and innovative outputs will result from this study?

Organizing the Research Plan

Organization of the research plan differs widely among writers and among disciplines. The goal is to keep the reader focused on the overall significance, objectives, and hypotheses while providing important methodological, technological, and analytical details. There are numerous ways to succeed at this. Here we provide two examples that we have encountered in effective grant applications.

MODEL 1. In this model, the overall research strategy and scope are presented in a short opening section in a paragraph or two. Typical titles are Research Design and Scope, Experimental Design, Research Protocols, and Strategic Plan. This section serves as a blueprint to keep the reviewer focused on the research objectives. It can be particularly helpful when organizing research plans comprising several distinct sections that require different methods and approaches (e.g., Study System, Sampling Program, Analytical Techniques, Field Experiments, etc.). Describe, at the start, your overall plan for linking these approaches.

Information must flow logically from the introduction and background sections. Provide evidence that your design is the best and most appropriate approach to solving the questions that you have identified as significant. Do not simply repeat what has already been said. Save space by including a table of key hypotheses, or a figure linking hypotheses and methods to specific objectives.

Some authors follow with a section on the specific methods—Methods and Materials, Experimental Protocols, and so forth. The order of presentation of methods should parallel the order in which the objectives and hypotheses are presented elsewhere in the text. Tables for complicated procedures may be helpful, and appropriate referencing to common methods is essential. Be sure to make clear which methods pertain to which questions or hypotheses. A third section will probably be necessary to provide details on statistical analysis of the data.

Model 1 Format for the Research Plan, Methods, and Analysis
> Research Plan
> 1. Overview of research plan and justification

2. Methods and materials
  —Sampling procedures
  —Culturing methods
  —Experimental protocol 1, 2, 3, etc.
  —Technical procedures, etc.
3. Data analysis

MODEL 2. In this model each objective and its associated hypotheses are presented with the study plan and methods that will be used to test them. For example, imagine that you have several objectives with their own derived hypotheses. In this format you present each objective separately, followed by the specific hypotheses and methods to examine them. This sequential approach can be effective in that each test follows directly from each question. However, in some cases you may find that you need to repeat material from previous methods, which may become tedious. With this format, authors may also include the analysis right after the methods section, eliminating the need for a separate section.

Model 2 Format for the Research Plan, Methods, and Analysis

Research Plan
1. Objective 1
Hypothesis 1A
  —Methods, materials, and protocol for H1A
  —Data analysis for H1A
Hypothesis 1B
  —Methods, materials, and protocol for H1B
  —Data analysis for H1B

2. Objective 2
Hypothesis 2A
—Methods, materials, and protocol for H2A
—Data analysis for H2A
Hypothesis 2B, etc.
—Methods, materials, and protocol for H2B
—Data analysis for H2B

What to Consider While Writing the Methods

Your research design and methods section is where you confirm for your readers that you have an achievable research plan. It is also where you highlight and defend innovative methods. Reviewers will carefully weigh this section in considering the pros and cons of the design. They will be asking questions like those that follow as they read your proposal.

Are these the correct and best methods for the specific questions? Perhaps the most decisive question that a reviewer will ask is whether the context and methods are the most fitting for meeting your objectives and testing your hypotheses. Although matching methods and objectives sounds simple, and it can be, some reviewers contend that inappropriate methodology is one of the most common flaws in unsuccessful proposals.

"I think I found your problem. You're putting in garbage."

Consider the following hypothetical example. An investigator proposed to measure the effects of aluminum on the reproduction and mortality of a particular species of fish. This author had convincingly argued the need for and value of this information, so reviewers were initially positive about the study. But as they read the design and methods section of the proposal they detected what became a fatal flaw for this study. The investigator planned to measure the total level of aluminum in fish tissue. Yet recent research had revealed that aluminum occurred in several chemical forms (species) in nature, and that not all forms were toxic to fish. Moreover, in some situations the toxic species of a metal has no relation to its total concentration. The reviewers concluded that the investigator would be making virtually meaningless measurements, and they now doubted the author's preparedness and understanding of current developments in the proposed field of study. In this simplistic example, the questions and hypotheses were sound, but poor methodology raised questions about the value of the work and the competence of the scientist, which resulted in a failed application.

Many other problems originate with a poor choice of methods, especially when there is no agreement in the field as to the best and most suitable ap-

proach. For example, the "best" (the fastest and most conclusive) procedures will generally be favored over others that also are feasible and workable, unless there is a serious drawback to their use. However, limited resources or access to particular instruments may prohibit your use of favored techniques. You may propose a less costly method for solving a problem, but it must be equally precise and reliable or reviewers are likely to object even if they are sympathetic to your plight. It would be beneficial to introduce the issues of cost of and access to new methods and technologies during the development of your ideas.

Are the methods proven and properly cited? Not all reviewers of your work will be experts in your field, so you must require evidence for the suitability of the proposed methods. Proper citation of established procedures and their application should suffice, eliminating the need to devote text to describing well-tried techniques. Innovative methodology and novel techniques can be highly regarded, but new or more controversial procedures require justification and affirming support. The most convincing support is documentation of their feasibility. We have submitted grant applications requiring adaptations or development of new techniques. These applications have been most effective

when we could provide preliminary data or calculations to suggest the likely success of the procedure. In one case the proposal was awarded a small amount of funding (5 percent of the request) specifically to generate preliminary data to demonstrate feasibility.

The need for preliminary data is a well-appreciated conundrum in science—you need some results before you can be funded, but you do not have funds to conduct the work until you receive the grant. Collaborating with scientists already generating results of the type you desire is one solution, and writing small development grants is another.

Are the methods feasible given the time and support available? There are other ways that flawed methodology can be the downfall of a proposal. For example, in some cases the methods may be feasible—they will do what you say they will do—but impractical. What you propose to do must be reasonable given your the time and resources.

Some people seem to feel that it is better to err on the side of proposing too much rather than too little. Graduate students often conceive projects that would require several dissertations to complete. While this may be acceptable to a tolerant graduate committee, a funding agency is unlikely to accept a serious mis-

match. Proposing too much casts doubt on your judgment, and it does not provide reviewers with information on how you prioritize the tasks. It is more effective
to educate the reviewers and convince them that you
can do what you say you will do. The timeline for a proposal (Chapter 11) may be scrutinized by reviewers for
this purpose.

*Is the precision or extent of the study appropriate
and sufficient to answer questions, hypotheses, or objectives?* When you have established that your questions
will be tested properly by your proposed methods, critical reviewers will assess the way you intend to handle
your data and conduct statistical analyses (see also
Chapter 10). An effective proposal demonstrates that
you understand and propose to use the best and most
powerful analytical techniques suited to your specific
experimental design, sample size, and replication. It
will be useful to consult with colleagues and advisers
about the data analysis. In some disciplines, mistakes
in data analysis are among the top reasons that a proposal fails to be funded.

*Are the investigators competent in the use of all
these techniques?* Reviewers will query whether you and
your collaborators have the technical expertise to accomplish the research. In most areas of study there are

laboratory techniques or field methods that are difficult, expensive, or time consuming. If you intend to
use these means, you must prove not only that they are
appropriate and feasible but that you are qualified to
use them. The testimony of people with whom you
have studied or trained, your preliminary data, and
your peer-reviewed publications will be used evaluate
your competence with a given technique or method. If
you are trying something novel and are also new to a
discipline, you may be unable to prove your skill in a
proposal. If so, you may wish to collaborate with someone who is well regarded in the field (Reif-Lehrer
1995). It may be enough to demonstrate that the "ex-
pert" has agreed to advise you or to conduct calibration
and cross-checking of samples, methodology, or techniques. A more formal collaboration (such as a subcon-
tract) may be best in circumstances where your ability
to conduct difficult work may be questioned. Many
agencies encourage multi-disciplinary collaboration,
and this is an excellent justification for working with
someone who complements your abilities.

   *What critical and innovative outputs will result
from this study?* Every effective proposal summarizes
the expected outputs from the study. It is common to
see proposals with a special section titled Expected Re-

sults (Chapter 10). The projected outputs of your study must be considered realistic and important. In some cases, investigators include a specific set of items that they will produce (a gene library, a collection of specimens, and new drug therapy), while others generate less tangible outputs (advancing our knowledge of a topic, testing an untested theory). Outputs should follow directly from the significance statements and in some sense address how the actual study is pertinent to the broadest stated goals. Be aware that reviewers may assess your work with this in mind.

Deciding What to Include

The methods and experimental design section of a research proposal differs from that of a manuscript in a fundamental way: proposals must include enough information for a reviewer to critically evaluate your methods, but they do not have to provide all the detail needed for someone to duplicate your work. There are times when you should list specific methods—particularly if you are relying on unpublished or novel procedures—but often it is appropriate simply to cite an earlier work or standard technique. Presenting too much information can diminish the punch of your proposal, but presenting too little may prompt readers to question your ability to conduct the work. Consultation with colleagues or even the program director at specific agencies can help you decide what is appropriate in your case. Just as you evaluate the contribution of each reference (Chapters 8 and 12), so should you question the need for each detail of your methods.

All proposals require a distinctive set of measurements or experiments, so it is not possible to produce a checklist of items for this portion of a research proposal. A few elements common to most methods sections are listed below; refer to proposals in your own area for more specific information.

Outline of proposed research. Most proposals include an outline or brief description of the overall methodological approach. This functions both as a road map and as a justification of your approach.

The study site, the species, the system. If your work depends on a certain organism, location, gene, model system, chemical product or process, or on a specialized piece of equipment, you should describe this here. Supply adequate information to allow the reader to understand the system in which your work will take place. This is especially important for reviewers who are not experts in your field. Discuss the background of the reviewers with the program director to determine how much detail to provide.

Methods. If your techniques are well known, it may suffice to write, "Collection and analyses will be conducted following the methods of So and So (1997)." If the methods are new, have been developed by you, or are not well known, thorough description and documentation are essential. Do the proposed methods have any particular limitations that might affect the interpretation of your results? Explicitly state those limitations and their implications. It is much better for you to point them out than for a reviewer to raise them.

Data analysis. If preliminary data are available, show how you will use or analyze them to reach your objectives or test your hypotheses. If such data are unavailable, consider culling data from the literature to show how you expect the results to turn out, and to show how you will analyze your data when they are available. Complete a table or diagram, or run some statistical tests using the preliminary or "synthesized" data. This can be a good way to show how you would interpret the results of such data (see also Chapter 10).

Sample/data storage and archiving; integrity of data. If appropriate, describe your intention to save, store, or archive physical samples or data (and any specific methods that you would employ). There are a number of situations in which this is beneficial. For example, you may be required by your funder to make data or samples available to other investigators. Even if these are not required, making your data accessible to other investigators may strengthen the proposal. You may also be planning a follow-up or comparison study. If so, maintaining the integrity of the samples or archived data base is critical.

Exercises for Writing the Methods Section

Critique other proposals. Once again, our first suggestion is that you critique other proposals in your immediate research area. Consider the extent to which they provide information and the way that it is presented. Act as a reviewer, using the questions listed above. Examine both successful and unsuccessful proposals, if possible. Unsuccessful proposals may provide some guidance on ineffective presentations or perceived weaknesses. Some authors may be willing to share samples of reviewers' comments from successful and unsuccessful proposals. Often the reviewers are explicit about the key weaknesses, which frequently occur in the methods and approach sections.

Critique these excerpts from the research design sections of two funded proposals.

Once the precise bases that interact with the gene APETALA3 (AP3) are identified, we plan to make specific base changes by site-specific mutagenesis (Kunkel et al. 1987). Once the mutations are made, we will clone them back into an otherwise wild-type AP3 promoter fused to β-glucuronidase (GUS). These constructs will then be transformed into the plant *Arabidopsis thaliana* and crossed to see whether they activate the GUS reporter. If single base changes destroy the ability of AP3 to autoregulate, that would provide convincing evidence that the mutated sequence mediates autoregulation.

Source: T. Jack

Within each section of stream we will survey three to four channel cross-sections (Feldman 1981) from valley side to valley side, for subsequent hydraulic modeling. Surveying will be accomplished with a Topcon AT-F6 automatic level. We will measure gravel sizes on riffles, channel area, pool area, and bar area using standard techniques and those of Wolman (1954) and Hankin and Reeves (1988). . . . The effects of channel bed roughness (primarily a function of bed particle size and slope) will be determined using empirical relationships determined by Jarrett (1985) for steep cross-sections typical of high-elevation streams.

Source: P. F. McDowell and F. J. Magilligan

EXERCISE 6. (This follows from the exercises given in Chapters 4 and 7.) Prepare a ten- to fifteen-minute oral presentation on the research design and methods for your research project. As in exercises 1–5, emphasize the relation of the study to the larger field of theoretical and empirical research preceding it. It will be difficult to do this in fifteen minutes, but by attempting it you will be forced to be succinct and precise. You may wish to undertake this drill several times, as logical flaws or poor presentations are revealed by feedback from colleagues or classmates. Soliciting comments from people in more peripheral disciplines can be especially helpful for distilling the jargon from your presentation.

After you work on your own methods section and research plan, seek comments on your written work. To help those giving you feedback, you may even suggest a list of questions (e.g., Is my description of how I will sample clear? Do you understand what I plan to do with the data?). After completing this section to your satisfaction, you have nearly completed your proposal. Your remaining tasks are much less momentous.

Plan for Expected and Unexpected Results

Strong scientific research proposals usually include a section following (or embedded within) the research plan; in this section the author presents the expected results and explicitly discusses their interpretation. However, even with the most carefully designed proposals one can face obstacles during implementation, or produce unexpected results that require rethinking original precepts, redesigning experiments, adding new or eliminating parts of original protocols.

In our surveys of colleagues, we were struck by the emphasis they placed on considering both likely and unlikely outcomes. They felt that investigators who are prepared to rapidly redirect research, or quickly respond to unusual yet important results, often produce the most exciting results. Science is filled with dramatic examples of a major breakthrough coming serendipitously through a failed experiment or as a

byproduct of an unrelated project. Therefore, we recommend that you also discuss unexpected or unlikely
outcomes along with expected results, and we offer a
few ways to address these issues in your proposal.

Explicitly Address Outcomes

Careful consideration of expected outcomes un-
derlies scientific competency and shows that the proposal authors are well prepared. Often the outcome of a
project or experiment is fairly predictable. This does
not mean that the research is stale or boring but may
simply indicate that the authors effectively established
hypotheses and models, examined the literature for applicable results from other systems, and perhaps were
just a bit lucky.

There are many ways to explicitly address outcomes in your proposal. Try several approaches.

- *Graphically depict the relationships you expect and
  discuss your analysis and interpretation.* Be sure
  to briefly discuss the interpretation that you
  will make if the patterns do not come out as
  predicted. State what such unexpected outcomes mean for your overall goal. In many
  cases, writers include fairly detailed descrip-

tions of the analysis necessary to interpret the
results. Attention to analysis can be especially
important when the analysis is novel, difficult,
quirky, or somewhat controversial.

• *Provide diagrams of the approaches you plan to use
for different outcomes.* If everything you propose
depends on one specific outcome, and that outcome does not occur, then the research will be
considered very risky. Make clear that each
pathway leads to valuable and interesting results. Although risky research is sometimes
necessary (i.e., when the gains are worth the
risk), when alternate outcomes all lead down
interesting pathways the research may be more
likely to succeed.

• *Construct a simulation model* to predict likely
outcomes (see also Chapter 8).

• *Estimate the likelihood that alternative outcomes
can result.* Some proposals include a table with
alternative hypotheses or outcomes. In certain
cases it is possible that the alternative requires
a mechanism that defies all logic. If so, little explanation may be needed, compared to a case
where two mechanisms are nearly equally plau-
sible. It is worth anticipating unlikely events, as

reviewers from different perspectives or disciplines may consider issues that you do not. By considering alternatives you may be able to identify aspects of your research that require special explanation for a broad audience.

Given other constraints on your proposal, your discussion of expected and unexpected results will probably be restricted to a few paragraphs or figures. The extent to which you need to discuss this depends in part on the ramifications of the different outcomes to your research design, hypotheses, and broader goals.

There is no consensus from authors and reviewers as to where this material should be located within the proposal. Some writers discuss results throughout the methods and hypotheses sections, while others place the discussion near the end of the body of the proposal. Sample titles for such sections include:

- Expected Results and Their Broader Significance
- Future Directions
- Related Research
- Model Limitation and Potentials
- Model Verifications

The Timeline Is a Reality Check

An organized and simple timeline is useful to both author and reviewer. Devising a timeline helps you acquire an appreciation for the links between tasks and for the time required for each part of the study, and insight into the resources (money and labor) required to complete the proposed project. This thinking process makes it more likely that you will budget correctly to successfully carry out the project. At the completion of a grant cycle you may decide to reapply for funds to continue your work. If you have underestimated the time and budget needed for the original project you will be in the position of justifying yourself in the new application.

Although the formal construction of the timeline is often left until after most other sections of a proposal have been written, it is best to think seriously about the time required for specific tasks while developing your research plan. A well-conceived timeline demonstrates to reviewers that you have carefully assessed the personal and financial commitments entailed by your project. A realistic timeline shows that the project is feasible and builds confidence in your judgment. If reviewers find the timeline overly optimistic they may have doubts about funding the proposal. Scientists with experience conducting the same type of research as you propose are your best sources of assistance in this area.

Constructing a Timeline

In NSF-formatted grants, the timeline usually appears at the end of the project description (see Chapter 9), just before the references. There are no blueprints for a timeline, but the start and finish of milestones in the project are usually depicted in chronological order. Sometimes authors simply list the general tasks and target dates, while others use more elaborate schematics. In general, the timeline is no more than one page long. If requirements for particular tasks need justification, include it in an accompanying paragraph.

Many different types of information are included, such as:

- the beginning and end of each field season or experimental period;

- time need to construct an instrument, pur-
chase new equipment, or develop a novel technique;

- time needed to create a genetic library, grow
particular cultures, etc.;

- time scheduled to use equipment at other facilities (e.g., telescope time, use of a mass spec-
trophotometer, sample deep-sea squid, etc.);

- starting and completion dates for a monitoring
program;

- when to expect publication of results.

No matter how carefully you plan your timeline, at some point "science and reality will meet," as a friend of ours says. All of us, even veteran researchers, can underestimate the time required for different tasks. A good guideline to follow is to make your best estimate of how long something will take and then double it. This still may not be enough time, but it may put you in the ballpark.

Here are two examples to consider before drafting your own timeline.

Sample 1

Timetable for a Fictional One-Year Study on
Amphibian Density and Respiration

JUNE 1999
- Order equipment.
- Receive, test, and calibrate equipment.
- Choose sites and test sampling methods.
- Install temperature monitoring stations.

JULY–OCTOBER 1999
- Collect continuous temperature data.
- Make weekly amphibian collections and measurements.
- Make monthly assessments of amphibian densities.

NOVEMBER 1999–MAY 2000
- Analyze data, perform statistical tests.
- Construct respiration/density model.
- Prepare papers for publication.
- Submit final report.

Sample 2

Timetable for a Four-Year Study on Extracellular and Intracellular Signals Regulation Cell Division and Differentiation

Projected Timetable	Year 1	Year 2	Year 3	Year 4
Cloning of *pex-1*	xxx	—	—	—
Molecular investigations of *pex—1* function	—	xxx	xxx	xxx
Genetic characterization of *pex—1*	xx	xx	xx	xx
Studies of spatial regulation of RAS-MAPK activity	—	xx	xx	xx
Screening for pachytene exit mutants	xxx	xxx	xxx	
Screening for suppressors/enhancers of RAS-MAPK	xxx	xxx	xxx	
Characterization of newly identified *pex* genes	x	xx	xx	xxx

Notes: — = done or not begun; x = low percentage effort; xx = moderate percentage effort; xxx = high percentage effort
Source: Excerpted from E. Lambie

References in Detail: How Many and How Recent?

Properly cited and appropriately chosen references are essential to a strong proposal. References alone will not determine whether a grant is funded, but weak use of citations suggests insufficient preparation and undermines confidence in an otherwise good application. Citations convey critical information to the reader with a minimum of words. Inexperienced writers sometimes have difficulty knowing how often and where to position references, and how to select among many possible choices. Below are guidelines for the judicious use of citations in a proposal and a review some of the more common referencing problems.

The Basics

Which references to cite? This is a fundamental question for authors of research proposals and manuscripts. The selections you make indicate a great deal about your perspective and knowledge of the current state in your field (see also Chapter 8). It is advisable to cite papers that are well known for their importance to a specific topic. References addressing your system directly and perhaps even your specific research question should also be used. We again emphasize the importance of being unbiased: cite papers that dispute your position and directly discuss the key differences in opinion. You should probably rely most heavily on recent papers, although in certain cases an older paper may still be considered the principal reference. In general, most cited papers will be less than ten years old, and inclusion of extremely recent references lends freshness to your application (and demonstrates that you keep current with the literature).

The conventions for citations in manuscripts also hold for proposals. For example, cite peer-reviewed works whenever possible. Use unreviewed work, reports, unpublished data, and personal communication sparingly. Cite your own work but not excessively.

Reviewers always weigh whether your proposal contains the most appropriate and consequential references. Be sure that the answer is yes (see Chapter 8). Consider who is likely to review your proposal (see Chapter 1). Remember that the scientists who will evaluate your study are probably doing some of the best and most relevant work, so it is reasonable to include one or more of their papers.

Finally, cite only papers that you have actually read. Occasionally writers lift lists of references from the text of other papers. This can be dangerous, as often the citations will not be relevant in even a slightly altered context. Reviewers do pick up on such carelessness. For example, we know of an author whose paper was incorrectly cited in a prominent publication. This author has found the wrong citation repeated numerous times in the literature.

How many references should I include? The typical answer—"You don't want more than you need, but be sure to have enough"—is vague. In general, cite all papers that are essential to establishing credibility or feasibility, but limit the use of citations that simply provide background and support. When establishing background, include the few most important or influential papers. Lists of more than five papers following a statement are rarely necessary. Do not use more references if one will suffice. Numerous citations for facts that are well appreciated in your discipline suggests naïveté on the part of the writer.

All citations should be accurate. Your references must be correct—pay particular attention to the date of publication. One of us was chastised for having a few references in the text that did not match the full citation at the end of the paper (i.e., the year of publication was not identical in both places). A reviewer wrote that since he or she was unable to see the data generated by the research, references were the only information that could be checked to determine whether the authors were likely to be careful and precise. The reviewer said that if a mistake in the citations was representative of the care we gave to our studies, our research may not be scrupulously done. A bit harsh (we thought!), but indicative of scientists' strong feelings regarding perceived sloppiness.

Common Problems

Here are some simple examples that illustrate how placement and number of references can lead to ambiguities. All references are fictional.

Too Many References, or References Are Too Vague

"Air pollution affects plants in a variety of ways (Browner and Bowles 1994, Kramer and Berger 1991, Smith and White 1993, Pearce and Omer, 1989, McPhee et al. 1996)." This is a vague statement to begin with, which makes it difficult to reference. It is not clear what the references in this list are supposed to indicate. If you use such open-ended statements, select only one or two general reviews for support.

"Air pollution affects plants in a variety of ways (e.g. Smith and White 1993)." This suggests that Smith and White is a review paper that discusses the many ways in which air pollution affects plants. If Smith and White present only one way in which air pollution affects plants, it is inappropriate to reference the statement this way.

References Placed Poorly in the Text

Some newer authors tend to place all references at the end of a paragraph when references may refer to different clauses within the paragraph. This can be very confusing and dilute the impact of the reference.

Note:

> While studies of the effects of vines on riparian
> plants have been conducted, there has not be an
> integrated analysis of the effect of vines on riparian
> plants (Asanti and Laszlo 1991, Schwartz et al. 1988,
> Jones and Smith 1995, Fullington 1977).

versus

> While studies of the effects of vines on plants in
> deltas (Asanti and Laszlo 1991, Fullington 1977),
> and estuaries (Schwartz et al. 1988, Jones and Smith
> 1995) have been conducted, there has not been an
> integrated analysis of the effect of vines on riparian
> plants.

The first sentence suggests that four studies identified
a need for an integrated analysis of the effects of vines
on riparian vegetation. In the second sentence, specific
studies in deltas and estuaries are cited. The absence of
a reference at the end of the sentence indicates that no
one prior to the author identified the lack of an integrated analysis of vines on riparian plants.

Weak or Incorrect References

By including a paper in your references you are
saying that you have read the paper and understood it
thoroughly. Cite it carefully, as authors are usually dis-
turbed when their work is referenced incorrectly.

Ambiguous Use of Reference Notation

Do not confuse references that are examples of your points with ones that support your argument in some other way, or make a similar point to the one you are making (e.g. = such as; i.e. = that is; cf. = confer).

Exercises for Writing References

There are several activities for preparing to choose references:

- Check the citation format for the agency to which you are applying.

- Develop a library of references for your proposal using packaged software.

Here is a simple drill. Read a paragraph written by a colleague or classmate in a field that is unfamiliar to you. Examine each reference and speculate on why it is there and what it should be telling you. Check with the author to see whether the intended message was correctly interpreted. This exercise is most effective when you are not familiar with the references cited. Apply the same consideration to your own citations.

Preparing a Budget

Most scientists write their budgets after completing the rest of their proposal. Whether you are applying to NSF for $250,000 or to your department graduate student fund for $250, there are some basic principles to follow when calculating your budget. The most important of these is to consider the ethics involved in accepting financial support for scientific research. You are obliged to follow the terms of the award, to include costs that relate directly to the research, and to take full responsibility for the veracity of your data and the appropriate use of the research dollars.

Budget writing requires careful planning and detailed knowledge of institutional administrative and overhead costs, and fairly precise estimates of equipment purchases, research assistant time, costs of supplies, and anticipated travel. For ethical and practical reasons, we suggest that you provide your most accurate estimate of the cost of conducting the research. Although some agencies are flexible in the extent to which they allow award costs to be transferred among categories as the research progresses, others are much stricter. In either case, the closer you follow your original budget, the better.

What Do I Include?

Preparing a budget is a process that gets easier with experience. All federal agencies, and most funding organizations, have a formal budget page for itemizing your budget into required categories. They are usually willing to provide detailed guidelines for particular costs. Discuss these issues with both your own campus grant office and the program director at the funding agency. Do this well in advance of the target date for submission, because getting a budget finalized and ready for submission to the funding agency can be complicated. Most agencies require a signed page including your signature and a signature of the individual at your institution responsible for the oversight of the funds. You may have to obtain the signatures of chairs, deans, and provosts before the institutional representative will sign your budget page.

In addition to the direct costs of conducting research, the so-called indirect costs, or overhead costs, must be included. Each institution negotiates these rates individually with most funding agencies, and so your campus will supply you with the specific indirect costs associated with different budget categories (e.g., salary, travel, supplies, etc.). Occasionally agencies set rates that differ from your institution's, and you will need to discuss this with your campus grant officer. In addition, most campuses charge different overhead rates for different types of research (e.g., off-campus versus on-campus activities). Last, most agencies restrict the overhead allowed on large equipment purchases. For all this information, contact your institution's grants office.

It is often necessary to include an additional page in which you justify in a few paragraphs certain budgetary requests. This budget justification page might explain why you need four thousand test tubes or sixteen trips to your field site during one field season. Here are a few of the most common budget categories.

- *Salaries*. People are expensive and research is labor intensive. For principal investigators, one-half, one, or two months of summer salary is typical. For other research staff, some number of calendar months should be indicated, depending on the percentage of a person's time that will be devoted to the project. Graduate stipends and undergraduate salaries are also often included. Each salary category carries different associated costs to cover benefits and overhead.

• *Equipment.* Most institutions and agencies have specific definitions of equipment (e.g., those items that cost more than $1,000 and will last more than one year). It is appropriate to include in your proposal equipment that is necessary to conduct the proposed work. However, if it is prohibitively expensive, it may limit your success. Any significant equipment expenditures should be discussed in advance with the program officer at the funding agency to determine their suitability. For large purchases, institutions and agencies will sometimes "cost-share" agreements, with both parties combining funds to purchase equipment. But plan in advance, because these arrangements must be finalized prior to submission, and they require time to negotiate.

• *Supplies.* Include all expendable items, including lab ware, chemicals and reagents, field utensils, and minor computer accessories necessary for the successful completion of your project.

- *Travel.* This category should include the destination and number of trips, the mileage, the cost for lodging, and a per diem for food. Justify all travel destinations (e.g., field sites, meetings with collaborators, conferences, outreach, patient reviews, etc.). Obtain your institutional guidelines for costs related to travel. It is common to include travel costs for presenting results of the study in later years of a project, but again each agency will have its own rules and restrictions.

- *Miscellaneous.* These costs include phone, postage, photocopying, and publishing. Discuss them with other people in your department to determine rules and common practices.

- *Subcontracts.* This category applies to cases where you plan to pay for work conducted at another institution. Again, local regulations will apply.

Final Thoughts on Preparing Budgets

Most scientist carefully estimate the true costs they expect to encounter while conducting research, and they submit a budget based on those realistic estimates. We strongly advise adopting this strategy. However, it is easy for those early in their careers to underestimate the amount of work involved and, consequently, to underestimate the amount of money needed. Caution, care, and consultation with senior colleagues or advisers are important. Preparing a fair budget not only will make your proposal more competitive, but it is the ethically appropriate strategy.

| | Itemization | |
Sample Budget for Field and Lab Study	Year 1	Year 2
Principal investigator		
1 month summer salary	$4,431	$4,652
Fringe benefits @ 18.2%	806	847
Postdoctoral research associate,		
full time	22,396	23,516
Fringe benefits @ 13.2%	2956	3,104
Graduate research assistant,		
full time	12,500	13,125
Fringe benefits @ 9%	1,125	1,181
Part-time laboratory technician,		
12 hours per week @ $8.93/hour	5,572	5,851
Fringe benefits @ 9%	502	527

Sample Budget for Field and Lab Study	Itemization	
	Year 1	Year 2
Summer field and lab assistant, 40 hours per week for ten weeks @ $6.50/hour	2,600	2,730
Fringe benefits @ 9%	234	246
Travel total	1,198	1,198
Ten trips to field site (80 miles round trip × $.31/mile)	248	248
Attend one conference	950	950
Supplies total	1,970	1,970
Reagents	225	225
Field sampling bottles, bags, and tools	440	440
Laboratory chemicals and containers	755	755
Analytical chemicals	550	550
Phone, postage, photocopying	250	263
Publication costs	800	800
Equipment	0	0
Total direct costs	57,340	60,010
Indirect cost @ 50%	28,670	30,005
Total budget	86,010	90,015
Total request for years 1 and 2:		$176,025

Submitting and Tracking Your Proposal

If you have finished your proposal, congratulations! You now have checked it for errors, typos, and formatting, and made certain that you followed the guidelines and rules of your institution and the funding agency. You've made the required number of copies (for some organizations it may be as many as twenty) or examined the guidelines for electronic submission. For NSF, all proposals submitted in the year 2000 and later must be prepared on their electronic proposal submission application program, called FastLane. FastLane lets you work on line, uploading sections of the proposal or typing them onto the electronic forms. When you prepare your individual budget pages using FastLane, it will calculate your summary budget. While NSF is the only agency of which we are aware that requires electronic submissions of proposals, many agencies are heading in that direction.

Our last suggestion is that you consider writing a cover letter. Not all agencies require it, but you are free to include one. In a brief cover letter you may wish to describe the importance of the work or discuss any previous dealings you may have had with the program director or panel. You can also provide names of individuals who may be suitable reviewers of your proposal. (None of these people should be collaborators, advisers, or advisees.) In rare cases it may be reasonable to include the name of a reviewer to avoid—if you have a specific reason. This information should be held confidential by the agency, but use the option sparingly. Most scientists never need to do this.

If submitting by mail, we strongly recommend that you use a service that will allow you to verify delivery. It is useful to know that your package arrived on time. It would be extremely unfortunate to go through all the work involved in preparing a proposal only to learn that it arrived after a deadline.

What Happens to Your Proposal After You Submit It?

Until the advent of electronic submissions, all proposals were received in the mailroom of the funding agency. Tens, hundreds, or even thousands of other submissions may have been received at the same time. Regardless of how a proposal is received today (through the mailroom or through e-mail), within a few weeks each proposal is assigned a number, and an acknowledgment of receipt bearing that number is sent to the author. Use this number in any correspondence regarding the proposal.

After a proposal is processed it will usually be sent to one or more individuals for review. Some agencies conduct in-house reviews. It is more common for the person responsible for evaluating grant proposals and making awards to assemble a list of ad hoc reviewers who will provide a written review of your proposal. Ad hoc reviewers have no formal association with the funding agency or its panels; they are members of the scientific community who agree to review a proposal. They perform a similar function to the ad hoc reviewers of manuscripts submitted to journals. Ad hoc reviewers are chosen many ways (e.g., from your citation section, from your cover letter, past contact with the agency, general standing in the field).

After the ad hoc reviews are received, many agencies arrange for the reviews to be evaluated by a panel consisting of scientists (often leaders in their fields, some of whom have received funds from that agency in the past) and members of the agency staff. For some U.S. federal agencies, several panel members read each proposal and write additional reviews that are added to the reviews submitted by ad hoc reviewers. A single panel member may be identified as the "primary" reader to present the major ideas of your proposal to the rest of the panel and comment on issues raised in the ad hoc reviews.

The panel discusses each proposal and generally writes a panel summary, which is a synopsis of the positive and negative aspects of the work. Panel members may also comment on the qualifications and productivity of the investigators. Proposals may then be ranked or placed in categories (e.g., "must fund," "possibly fund," "don't fund"). The program director generally makes the final decisions on funding and notifies investigators about the outcome of their proposal. Most agencies say when decisions will be made, and it is rarely a good idea to call the agency prior to this date. Many agencies do not make final decisions until four, five, or even six months after the deadline for submission.

People receiving good news usually receive it first, perhaps within a week or two of the decision, and usually by phone. Bad news comes more slowly, usually by post or electronic mail. Eventually you should receive a set of reviews of your proposal and a written panel summary. But we urge you to call the agency for feedback on failed proposals rather than wait for this packet, which can take months to arrive. We suggest calling the agency any time after the decision date.

If your proposal was funded, congratulations! If not, *don't despair.* In this era of limited funding and highly competitive programs, many proposals are not funded on their first submission. You will probably wish to revise and resubmit your proposal to the same agency. Careful consideration of the panel summary is an important part of the resubmission process.

The Three R's:
Rethink, Revise,
and Resubmit

Do not be too disappointed if your proposal is rejected the first time it is submitted. This is not uncommon, and a revised proposal is usually much stronger. Some granting agencies provide you with several ad hoc reviews and a written summary of the panel deliberations. Consider yourself lucky if you receive a large number of reviews; it is a great advantage to receive copious feedback on your research. All scientists benefit from reviewers' comments and insightful critiques. Successful grant writers use these comments to revise and improve their plan.

Research proposals are rejected for many reasons, and even some very good proposals go unfunded. To better your chances the second time around, consider seriously each suggestion from the program director, agency head, or review panel. Remain open-minded—you do not need to agree with them or adopt all of their suggestions, but at least be prepared to support your viewpoint in the next version. Below are general strategies for rethinking and revising your proposal. Your close colleagues or advisers can advise you about responses to the more specific comments.

Significantly Improving the Resubmission

Many of us spend hundreds of hours on our proposals, so it is difficult to receive a rejection, particularly when the grant you have labored long to produce is brushed off in a few paragraphs. It is not unusual to feel that a reviewer or even the entire panel misunderstood something you wrote. Experiences like these can be useful if you take the position that they did not understand because *you* did not make your point clearly. Let your disappointment, anger, and frustration subside before you rethink and revise your proposal. By being as objective as you can you will improve the chances of getting your proposal funded upon resubmission.

Evaluate reviewers' comments. Begin by reading your proposal from start to finish. It has probably been a few months since you last read it, so you will see it with fresh eyes. Look again at the reviewer comments. As you examine each remark, try putting it into one of the following categories: "must consider," "may consider," "ignore."

If you feel that all of the comments belong in the third category, you are probably not accepting criticism very well. But if the concerns are distributed among all three, or are primarily in the first two categories, you are off to a good start. Review the comments from the first two categories and identify the sections of the proposal to which they are most pertinent. Observe the patterns that arise. For example, you may notice that a large number of issues deal with your methods or hypotheses. Or you may find that most concerns relate to the scope of your project. This exercise will help give you a feeling for which sections of your proposal need the most serious revision or were least clearly expressed.

Edit your proposal. The extent to which you need to rethink, revise, and rewrite differs for every proposal. Our rule of thumb is to adopt a strategy similar to that used to conceive and draft your original proposal.

- Start with the big questions: Were they clear? Did the reviewer accept their significance? Were the links between your broadest goals and your proposed research plan convincing? If these areas received the greatest criticism you'll need to rethink your proposal from the fundamental tenets.

• Funnel downward to the specifics of your research plan. Determine whether your discussion led to misunderstandings in the methods. Did you overlook important papers that could alter your research design? Did you make any mistakes in analysis or interpretation? Did you omit a key set of experiments that could change your final product?

• Look for strategic errors that could have affected the reviews. Were you unrealistic in your timeline? Did you fail to highlight key points, or did you overwhelm them so that they were lost? Was your budget out of line?

• Discuss the criticisms and your responses with colleagues.

Finally, remember that reviewers sometimes make suggestions that are not tenable or are off the mark, but if you follow this process you should be able to substantially improve your proposal. You have an important added advantage over your first submission—you now know what some of the reviewers' concerns are likely to be. Make use of this information in your revision. It can only help.

Writing a Resubmission Response

In the past few years it has become common to include a resubmission response in revised proposals. Some agencies even require a response to prior reviews. A resubmission response should be no more than a few paragraphs. Summarize the major comments made by the reviewers (positive as well as negative), and describe how these comments were incorporated into the revision or why you chose not to incorporate them.

A resubmission response is valuable for a number of reasons. First, it allows the author to carefully consider each reviewer comment and to check your response to it. Second, it guarantees some institutional memory for your proposal. If the initial reviewers agreed that you wrote an excellent proposal and that the only major weaknesses were in the methods, you should remind the panel of this in your revised submission. This response puts some pressure on the agency to acknowledge the previous review, even if there are new program officials and reviewers of the revised proposal. Third, it draws attention to the improvements you have made.

Since the resubmission response is a fairly new component of most proposals, there is not a consensus on the best location. Some investigators place it at the beginning of the project description, and others place it at the end, just before the references. You may also place it in your cover letter. If this is a strong statement, and if it can be used to highlight key points or deflect key sources of potential concern, placing it early may be advantageous.

Ethics and Research

You accept substantial implicit and explicit responsibility when you conduct scientific research. If you accept financial resources to fund your research, you are fully accountable to your institution, the scientific community, and the funding agency. As one who enjoys the privilege of conducting science, you have a responsibility to society to hold yourself to strict moral and ethical standards (Shrader-Frechette 1994).

In this chapter we bring up a few topics related to ethics that should be understood by all graduate students, faculty, and investigators involved in scientific research. We urge you take a class or participate in a seminar or reading group on this subject at some point in your career. Most research institutions offer such courses, and certain funding agencies require that their recipients complete one. Some stimulating books on ethics in science are included in Appendix I.

Issues to Ponder

Many ethical issues can arise when one is conducting scientific research with public or private funds. Many of these, such as proper citation techniques, ownership of ideas, and budgetary oversight, have been discussed in other chapters. Here we identify four general areas in which ethical standards must be maintained. Reflecting on these vital aspects of conducting research is a healthy exercise. Open discussion with students and collaborators is of obvious scientific benefit at all phases of research proposal development and implementation.

Give appropriate credit. As you write your proposal, and as you present your ideas to others informally or in presentations, be careful to recognize the contributions of others. It is always appropriate to acknowledge that certain ideas in your proposal derive from the work of others. As we discussed earlier, giving appropriate credit can lead to more complicated issues, such as authorship and scientific oversight for the integrity of the data. Early, frequent, and open communication will significantly reduce the possibility of dis putes among investigators.

Respect people, animals, plants, and the environ-ment. It is vital to respect the people, organisms, and the environment when conducting research. In recent years federal, state, and institutional regulations to en-sure this have become common. All academic institu-tions have committees that routinely review research involving human subjects and animals. Many funding agencies require specific information on animal care and maintenance to be included in the grant applica-tion (see Chapter 3). However, even if your research does not fall under these regulations, you should work to ensure that your activities have the minimum im-pact possible. A discussion of this with colleagues could be useful, especially for beginning researchers and graduate students.

Remain objective. We doubt that anyone starts out with the intention of falsifying data. Yet severe sci-entific misconduct does occur, and it is always devastat-ing to the scientific community. Less deliberate or in-advertent mishandling of data does occur more frequently, but all efforts to avoid this should be made as well. For example, a researcher may become so con-vinced of the outcome of an experiment that he or she ignores or dismisses contradictory results. Or an investigator may choose to conduct experiments that favor particular outcomes. By remaining objective, the chance of biasing your results will be greatly reduced. Although scientists have many ways to ensure the validity of research (e.g., peer review, publishing results and data), problems still may arise. By being open about your studies, sharing your ideas and research designs, encouraging and soliciting criticism, and being self-critical, you can ensure your own objectivity throughout your research career.

Spend money appropriately. Accepting financial support for research constitutes an agreement that you will spend the award money on the approved research and that you will follow all guidelines for reporting your use of funds. Different agencies have different regulations concerning the shifting of money from one budget category to another. Deviations from the original, approved budget often require explanation, justification, and permission. Expenditures on nonresearch items, or wasteful spending, are *not* permissible. Financial misconduct is never tolerated, regardless of intent, so we encourage you to maintain a close relationship with your granting officer and to ask questions whenever you are unsure of regulations.

Use the Guidance and Advice of Others

Our strongest recommendation is that whenever you have ethical questions—whether you are a first-year graduate student or an experienced researcher—the best approach is to talk to colleagues and mentors in your field. Discuss your potential difficulties with those you respect, and you will almost certainly avoid seeing them become real dilemmas.

Appendix 1
Additional Reading

Grant Applications, Research, and Writing

Davidson, C. I., and S. A. Ambrose. 1994. The New Professor's Handbook. Anker, Bolton, Mass.

Day, R. A. 1988. How to Write and Publish a Scientific Paper (3rd ed.). ISI Press, New York.

Hailman, J. P., and K. B. Strier. 1997. Planning, Proposing, and Presenting Science Effectively. Cambridge University Press, Cambridge.

Katz, M. J. 1985. Elements of the Scientific Paper. Yale University Press, New Haven.

Locke, D. 1992. Science as Writing. Yale University Press, New Haven.

Matthews, J. R., J. M. Bowen, and R. W. Matthews. 1996. Successful Scientific Writing. Cambridge University Press, Cambridge.

Penrose, A. M. and S. B. Katz. 1998. Writing in the Sciences. St. Martin's, New York.

Reif-Lehrer, L. 1995. Grant Application Writer's Handbook. Jones and Bartlett, Boston.

Spencer, C. M., and B. Arbon. 1996. Foundations of Writing. National Textbook Co., Lincolnwood, Ill.

Ethics in Science and Research

Altman, E., and P. Hernon. 1997. Research Misconduct. Ablex, Greenwich, Conn.

Elliott, D., and J. E. Stern (eds.). 1997. Research Ethics. University Press of New England, Hanover, N.H.

Shrader-Frechette, K. 1994. Ethics of Scientific Research. Rowman and Littlefield, Boston.

Stern, J. E., and D. Elliott. 1997. The Ethics of Scientific Research. University Press of New England, Hanover, N.H.

Problem Solving and Creativity

Moriarity, S., and T. Duncan. 1995. Creating and Delivering Winning Advertising and Marketing Presentation (2nd ed.). National Textbook Co., Lincolnwood, Ill.

Runco, M. A. (ed.). 1994. Problem Finding, Problem Solving, and Creativity. Ablex, Norwood, N.J.

Web Addresses for Funding Organizations

American Chemical Society: *http://www.acs.org/acsgen/prf/grant.htm*

AT&T Foundation: *http://www.att.com/foundation/search.html*

Carnegie Corporation of New York: *http://www.carnegie.org/*

Charles A. Dana Foundation: *http://www.dana.org/*

Department of Agriculture National Research Initiative Competitive Grants Program (USDA Competitive Grants): *http://www.reeusda.gov/nri/*

Department of Education: *http://gcs.ed.gov/grntinfo.htm*

Department of Energy: *http://www.doe.gov/*

Earthwatch Institute–Center for Field Research: *http://www.earthwatch.org/cfr/cfr.html*

Environmental Protection Agency: *http://www.epa.gov/docs/ord/*

European Grants Limited:
http://www.europeangrants.com/

Funding Database Index: *http://www.omhrc.gov/new-fund.htm*

John Simon Guggenheim Memorial Foundation:
http://www.gf.org/

Heinz Endowments: *http://www.heinz.org./*

John D. and Catherine T. MacArthur Foundation:
http://www.macfdn.org/

Andrew W. Mellon Foundation: *http://www.mellon.org/*

National Aeronautics and Space Administration:
http://www.nasa.gov/newsinfo/research.html

National Institutes of Health: *http://www.nih.gov/*

National Science Foundation: *http://www.nsf.gov/*

NATO Scientific and Environmental Affairs Division:
http://www.nato.int/science/

Office of Naval Research: *http://www.onr.navy.mil/*

Alfred P. Sloan Foundation: *http://www.sloan.org/*

United States–Israel Binational Science Foundation:
http://www.bsf.org.il

References

Published Works

Day, R. A. 1988. How to Write and Publish a Scientific Paper (3rd ed.). ISI Press, New York.

Gilpin, M. E., and M. E. Soulé. 1986. *In* Conservation Biology (M. E. Soulé, ed.). Minimum Viable Populations: Processes of Species Extinction. Sinauer Associates, Sunderland, Mass., pp. 19–34.

National Science Foundation. Grant Proposal Guide. NSF 99–2, October 1998.

Reif-Lehrer, L. 1995. Grant Application Writer's Handbook. Jones and Bartlett, Boston.

Runco, M. A. (ed.). 1994. Problem Finding, Problem Solving, and Creativity. Ablex, Norwood, N.J.

Shrader-Frechette, K. 1994. Ethics of Scientific Research. Rowman and Littlefield, Boston.

Unpublished Proposals

Ambros, Victor R.

Black, P. N.

Boyce, Richard L., and Andrew J. Friedland.

Folt, Carol L., Celia Y. Chen, Richard S. Stemberger.

Friedland, Andrew J.

Jack, Thomas P.

Kirk, Kevin D.

Eric J. Lambie.

McDowell, Patricia F., and Frank J. Magilligan.

McLaughlin, D. W., and R. Shapley.

Miller, Eric K., Andrew J. Friedland, and Joel D. Blum.

Morel, François M. M.

Parker, D. D.

Sloan, Lisa C.

Tyson, J. J.

Index